Closer Apart
by John Monks & Lizzie Shupak

#closerapart
www.closerapartbook.com

PRAISE FOR CLOSER APART

"*Closer Apart* is the definitional guide this space sorely needs. It's comprehensive, witty and bursting with the kinds of everyday hacks I'm after. Most importantly, as with everything Lizzie and John do, there is a fiercely human, holistic perspective that shoots through its every pore."

Jack Fryer, Managing Director, The Square @ Universal Music

"*Closer Apart* will be a game changer for facilitators, who'll learn from two grand masters of the profession."

Jochen Menges, Leadership Scholar at the Universities of Zurich and Cambridge

"Bringing people together should be everyone's job. It's how great things happen. Whether or not you think of yourself as a facilitator, this book will help you to help others be awesome."

Michael Bungay Stanier, bestselling author of *The Coaching Habit* and *The Advice Trap*

"Everything I've learned in 20 years of in-person and online workshops and wish I had written down is in here. *Closer Apart* will not only make your online workshops more successful, but more enjoyable to facilitate, too. Happy online workshopping!"

Pam Hamilton, Paraffin MD and Author of *Supercharged Teams* and *The Workshop Book*

"Truly the best book of the year for me, and for anyone who's trying to greet this new Future of Work head-on, with zest. It will help you get the full participation of everyone whose contribution matters, and whose voice needs to be part of our path forward."

Andrea Kates, author of *Find Your Next* and *Futureproofing: Next.* Founder of Get To Next

"An essential tool for making online workshops engaging and impactful."

Mark Vernooij, Partner at THNK School of Creative Leadership

"The way we work has changed dramatically, and with that change comes the need for new skills. *Closer Apart* bridges the gaps many of us now face as we adjust to new ways of working."

Gethin Nadin, MBPsS, award-winning psychologist and bestselling HR author

"I loved this book. A super-practical guide to creating engaging, human, and, most importantly, effective virtual experiences. There's something for everyone, whether you're just getting started or looking to improve on a successful approach... read it!"
Tim Sparke, Founder of Congregation.io & The Friday Club London

"Facilitating groups to collaborate meaningfully has never been more valuable. When collaborations are so often fraught with hierarchy and politics, *Closer Apart* reminds us that we are all human beings, with our own needs, perspectives and unique contributions to make."
Dee Poku, Founder and CEO, The WIE Site

"In the past year, the shift from in-person to online workshops and conferences has often been a clumsy translation. John and Lizzie's necessary and excellent hands-on guide heightens the experience and learning for online attendees. I'll be using it as a reference for all my future online events."
Jon Jachimowicz, Assistant Professor of Business Administration, Harvard Business School

"Only creativity and collaboration can solve the big challenges of our time. *Closer Apart* combines brilliant insights with practical tools to help you train, shape, and harness your true facilitation power."
Adam Murphy, Experience Director, Philips

"*Closer Apart* is a fantastic refresher on how to run workshops in any situation. Full of practical tips, it will help facilitators and groups working remotely to create energy and deliver high-impact sessions."
Gerald Breatnach, Head of Strategic Insights, Google UK

"There's much talk today about being inclusive in the workplace. *Closer Apart* actually guides you to design experiences that bring the best out of everyone and help people create together - even when they aren't. A great reminder of the value of thoughtful facilitation."
Sameer Modha, Client Strategy Data & Effectiveness Lead, ITV

"Clear, concise, beautifully illustrated and utterly brilliant."
Prof. Dr. Jane Lê, Otto Beisheim School Of Management

"*Closer Apart* will help you feel well-prepared and in control, even in the face of the many unexpected challenges that regularly appear in a technologically driven environment. It challenges the idea that online workshops are difficult and dreary, and explores their exciting true potential."

Moulsari Jain, Senior Faculty, The School of Life

"Skilling has to be learnt in bite-size pieces and that's how *Closer Apart* is designed. You can go back and forth focussing on what you need to know at the moment, and then come back to the rest. I loved its little nuggets of wisdom, given throughout in the form of tips."

Shyama V. Ramani, Professorial Fellow, United Nations University-MERIT, Maastricht (NL) and Founder-Director of Friend In Need India Trust

"This is my new bible for facilitating online workshops and will forever be to-hand on my desk."

Paola De Marchi, Director of Learning and Development, Publicis Groupe

"*Closer Apart* is one of the rare business books that encapsulates the moment we are in. This clear, easy-to-read guide on how to build interactive workshops with empathy and soul is a must-read."

Laura Mignott, CEO of DFlash

"In *Closer Apart*, John and Lizzie bring all their experience and expertise in facilitation to bear, showing us how we too can become expert online facilitators.

Cain Ullah, Chair of Red Badger and CEO of Mission Beyond

"An utterly brilliant read. We've used many of the top tips to successfully facilitate transformation workshops at Bacardi. *Closer Apart* is a real 'facilitator's bible' for anyone dealing with the new normal."

Steve Paler, Global Director of Digital Transformation, Bacardi

A beautiful book for Beautiful Business, *Closer Apart* gives you practices and approaches that produce excitement, help people connect as humans and let new ideas flourish.

Tim LeBrecht, Co-Founder and Co-CEO, House of Beautiful Business

Closer Apart

ISBN: 978-1-7399557-0-0
Published by Curve Creative

First Edition
First published in 2021

Illustrations by Lizzie Shupak
Cover and Interior Design by Hazel Graham
Editing by Cate Caruth
Copy-Editing by Anthea Morrison

For more on Curve visit **www.curve.cc**

MARK PRINCE, MANAGING DIRECTOR
GLOBAL HEAD OF BRAND AT ACCENTURE

BEFORE COVID-19 struck in 2020, few companies had seriously considered a situation in which every employee would need to be enabled to work remotely, full time. Enforced lockdowns challenged our beliefs that some work needed to happen in person, and crushed orthodoxies that certain activities, such as planning meetings, creative and strategic ideation, and even pitching to clients, would never work virtually.

The global pandemic has changed the way we work forever. We've discovered that virtual ways of working, when designed well, can deliver experiences at the same level or sometimes drive even more engagement. However, just moving an in-person meeting to an online platform like Microsoft Teams doesn't automatically make it more efficient, effective, or enjoyable —

although it can be all three. Virtual meetings also give us the chance to hide, to observe rather than participate, to be distracted by other work—or to give in to the snacks calling our name from the pantry.

It became clear to me that for virtual meetings to succeed, we had to intentionally design them to maximize participation, keep people's attention and make sure everyone contributes. By leaning into our people's human ingenuity and several virtual collaboration tools, we made meetings more effective and equitable, accelerated towards our 2025 goal of net zero by reducing travel and CO_2 emissions, and helped protect people's time at home as they learned to juggle the demands of the pandemic.

But the right technology alone can't drive the meaningful experiences we need to ensure a truly connected workforce.

Also essential is a skilled and experienced facilitator who can help drive higher equality, effectiveness and engagement in the most important meetings and workshops.

In *Closer Apart*, John and Lizzie show us that expertly run virtual workshops are the key to thriving in this new world, and that we can do all the things we used to do in person just as well, and arguably even more effectively, in an online setting. It might come as a revelation to readers that with the right skills and approach, it's possible to design a workshop where a team can collaborate and meet its objectives in a session lasting just two hours.

I've had the pleasure of working with John and Lizzie for many years. I've gotten to know a lot of world-class facilitators, but Lizzie and John bring something unique to their workshops: a rare combination of energy, insight and in-depth understanding of what encourages and inhibits collaboration. They continue to mentor me and my teams because there's always room for improvement.

Closer Apart shares the secrets of successful online facilitation in an accessible and engaging way, drawing on real-world examples and offering practical tools. You can start small, practice to gain confidence and then add another simple activity, gradually expanding towards much bigger outcomes. It's ultimately a book for facilitators who want to stand out from the crowd. If you're curious; if you're someone who likes to push your thinking a little bit further; if you want to take your online workshops to a different level, this is a book you can't afford to be — or meet — without.

"

In life, there is no such thing as impossible; it's always possible.

VENUS WILLIAMS

"

ABOUT THE AUTHORS

AFTER many years of working and running workshops together, John Monks and Lizzie Shupak co-founded their creative leadership company, Curve. Their separate facilitation journeys began way back when Lizzie was volunteering in youth groups and John was working for his university's student union. This shared passion for bringing people together to generate new ideas has driven and inspired them throughout their careers. John went on to facilitate large change programmes, create new organisational models for digital businesses and train as a coach. Lizzie used her facilitation skills to help start-ups imagine and launch new ideas, and to help global brands with

innovation for new digital products and services. At Curve, Lizzie and John work together to pioneer new ways for people to collaborate and co-create online. Their staunch belief in the potential for people to come together more inclusively, more sustainably and more successfully online, is what led them to write this book.

PART 01

PART 02

PART 03

00.

Introduction

Why read this book

Learn from the experts

This book is for you if:

How this book works

WHY READ THIS BOOK?

WHAT comes to mind when you think about
online workshops? These are some of the
responses we often hear:

The introductions are really awkward

It's so tiring watching and listening to people on my screen all day

Everyone seems to suffer from energy slumps

Sound familiar? We've written this book to show you that online workshops don't have to be like this. Once you've mastered the skills of facilitating online, your remote workshops will be more enjoyable and get better results than in-person sessions. Yes,

you heard us right! After you've read this book, you'll be able to run online workshops that will have your participants buzzing with energy and enthusiasm as you unleash their potential and get them thinking, creating and collaborating like never before.

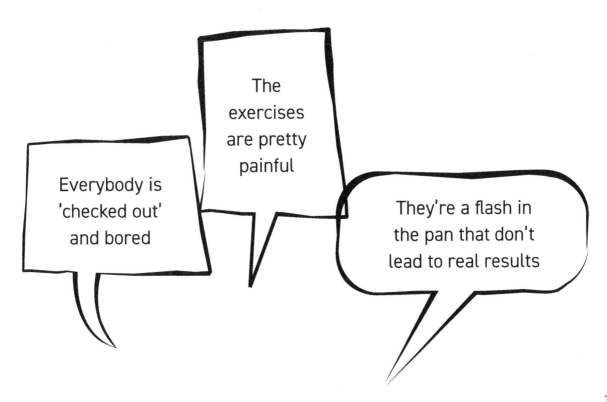

LEARN FROM THE EXPERTS

WE'VE run countless workshops over the past two decades, both online and in person. We've facilitated on every online platform, and on every continent inhabited by humans (we're still pitching to the penguins). Our participants range from first responders in New York City, to students tackling public transport problems in Moscow, to tech giants in Dubai. We've worked with fledging start-ups and with the United Nations; with Coca-Cola and with Comic Relief.

We developed our Curve training programmes to share what we've learned with others, helping hundreds of facilitators guide their participants to the results they need through the power of online workshops. We've shown them, and now we're going to show you, that, equipped with the right skills, everyone can design and run brilliant workshops online.

We'll share our tried and tested approach for designing and planning workshops, from setting the outcomes and selecting the tools, to managing energy levels and helping your participants get the most out of their experience. We'll walk you through every step of the process, from the planning stages, through the day itself, to the follow-up activities. As well as sharing the powerful techniques and tools that we use in our own practice, we'll introduce you to talented facilitators, innovators, coaches and change-makers who'll share their own approaches and tools to inspire you. Equipped with all this knowledge, you'll have the confidence to go out into the world and deliver your own outstanding workshops.

THIS BOOK IS FOR YOU IF:

- You need to plan and deliver a specific online workshop
- This is your first workshop or you've facilitated a few workshops before
- You're experienced in facilitating in-person workshops and want to take them online
- You've tried facilitating online but didn't get the results you wanted
- You're looking for new tips and techniques to enhance your skills

The exercises in particular assume that you're planning an upcoming workshop, so keep this book close to hand and refer back to it every time you have a workshop to design.

HOW THIS BOOK WORKS

BEFORE we get started, we want to tell you how we've structured the book and suggest how to get the most out of it.

Part One explores what makes the workshop such a powerful tool, how workshops came about and where they're headed. We'll consider the many advantages of online over in-person workshops and why it's useful to look at every workshop, and your progress through the book, as a journey.

Part Two takes what we consider to be the 'four pillars' of the online workshop – Technology, Facilitator, Participants and Energy – and explores the key considerations for each one when designing and running your workshop.

Part Three is where we delve into the nuts and bolts of preparing, designing and running your workshop, step by step. This is the section you'll likely refer back to the most as you plan your own workshops.

LEARN BY DOING!

From the graph on the next page, you can see that the more you interact with new knowledge through teaching it, watching it, practising it and talking about it, the more likely you are to retain it. Reading alone is the least effective way to learn and retain knowledge. That's why we always use a workshop setting – real or virtual – for our training programmes.

HOW MUCH WE REMEMBER
DEPENDS ON HOW WE LEARN

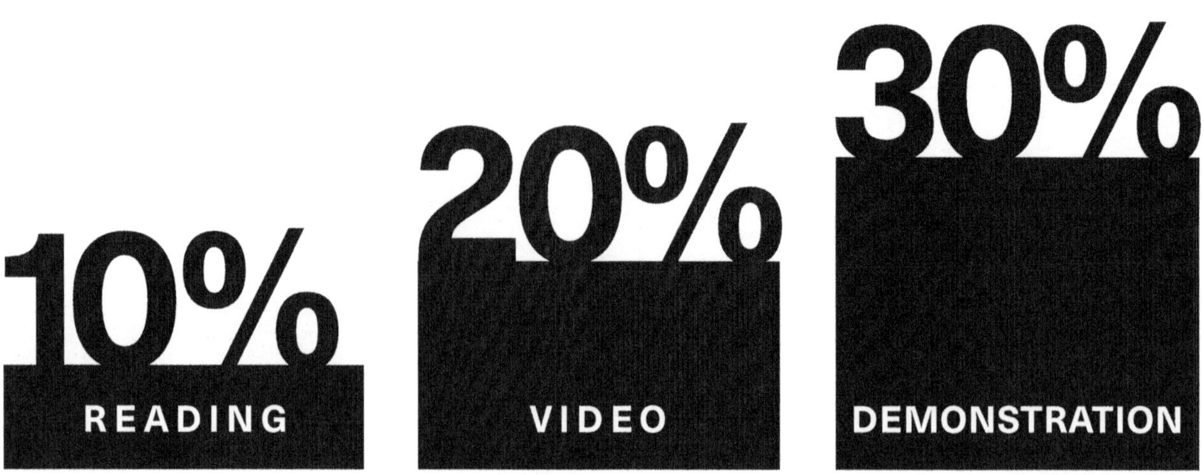

10% READING

20% VIDEO

30% DEMONSTRATION

50%

DISCUSSION

75%

PRACTICE

90%

TEACHING
OTHERS

BEFORE YOU GET STARTED

WE'VE written this book to replicate the workshop experience as far as possible. For you to get the most out of it, we're asking you to go beyond just reading and immerse yourself in the whole experience it offers you.

Watch the spotlight videos as you work through the book, by visiting the Closer Apart website at www.closerapart.com. We'll often refer you to the website, so bookmark it now.

Complete the exercises and reflection prompts, even if you have to imagine a workshop you're planning for now. We've provided spaces for you to write notes but if

you don't like the idea of writing in a book, you can use your own notebook our journal to complete the exercises.

Visit the Closer Apart website to join our facilitator community via the website and ask questions and share your experience. Talk to colleagues and friends about what you've learned. All this will help you absorb and retain your new knowledge for when you need it in action.

Use the QR codes whenever we refer you to the Closer Apart website to watch a spotlight video, find further resources or download a planning canvas to fill in – they'll take you straight to what you need.

CLOSER APART WEBSITE:
Find us here, ask questions
and share your experience.

TERMINOLOGY

A NOTE on the terms we use in the book. We refer to workshops as being 'in person' when participants are together physically and 'remote' or 'online' when participants are in different locations connected via their internet devices. Where some people are together in one physical space and others are online, we refer to this as a 'hybrid' workshop.

SPOTLIGHT ON

Director of Virtual not Distant
PILAR ORTI

Talking about
REMOTE WORKING

YOUR JOURNEY

IMAGINE this book as a journey. When you reach your destination you'll have everything you need to facilitate a brilliant online workshop. We'll be by your side as you navigate your way through the chapters, cheering you on as you discover the tools and skills you need. Guest facilitators will join for parts of the journey and inspire you with fresh perspectives. Travelling as a group, we'll experience lots of aha moments along the route, when the clouds part and the sun shines a whole new light on problems you've previously grappled with alone in the dark. From these lofty peaks of enlightenment you'll be able to see the broad plains of opportunity spread out before you. You'll have the chance to pause and sit for a while in quiet sunny glades where you can take stock and reflect on your experiences. Finally, we'll lead you to a launchpad at the end of the road, watch you step confidently into your rocket, and wave you off as you soar away to deliver your own brilliant remote workshops.

Ok, so we might have overdone it a bit with the metaphor, but hopefully you can see the parallels we're drawing between reading this book and the workshop experience. Using the journey metaphor is a simple, powerful way to describe the flow of a workshop to your participants, illustrating how working together as a team through the different stages and exercises will get them to their desired destination.

THE POWER OF YET

YOU'LL get the most from this book if you approach it with an open and positive frame of mind. Have you ever thought about trying something new in a workshop but when the moment came, you decided to just stick to something you know? That could have been an opportunity missed. Carol S. Dweck coined the term, 'Growth Mindset' in her book, *Mindset*. She explains that what you learn and what you achieve is largely determined by how you think. If you approach something excited to learn and believing you can achieve it, you probably will. This is a growth mindset. If you believe you're not capable - that your abilities are fixed – you probably won't try and you're much less likely to succeed. This is a fixed mindset. The table below shows the characteristics of the two mindsets. Choose the growth mindset!

GROWTH MINDSET	FIXED MINDSET
Embraces challenges	Avoids challenges
Learns from criticism	Ignores feedback
Pushes through challenges	Gives up easily

FACILITATOR TIP:
When participants tell you why
they believe something is
impossible, or reasons it won't work,
try summarising their thoughts back
but add the word 'yet' to the end.
"We can't do that," becomes
"we can't do that yet," changing it
from a blocker to an invitation.

My body achieves what my mind believes.

TOM DALEY

EXCERCISE 1 – REFLECTING ON GREAT WORKSHOPS

Think about workshops you've been to in the past.

What made them great? What were the features and exercises? How did the facilitator interact? Was it about the tools you used, the way the agenda was presented?

01.

The future of workshops

Why do we need workshops?

Where do workshops come from?

Where are workshops going?

Anything is possible!

Easier, Better, Faster, Cheaper

PART 01

WHY DO WE NEED WORKSHOPS?

Over the last few decades, the workshop of centuries past has evolved to take on a very different meaning in the modern world of work.

Since the start of the global pandemic, it's evolved again, showing us the infinite possibilities we can achieve when we work together to apply our uniquely human attributes of creativity, imagination and invention.

WHERE DO WORKSHOPS COME FROM?

THINK about the spaces where craftspeople used to make furniture or watches. They were physical places where skilled people would come to put their creative skills to work; where customers would come to view the products, try them out and shop.

In the twentieth century, 'workshop' became a verb as well as a noun, describing people working with their minds; creating thoughts more than physical things. On Manhattan's Madison Avenue, the copywriters, illustrators and designers portrayed through the fictional characters of TV's 'Madmen' series, joined forces to find novel ways of selling everything from beans to booze. Their real-world equivalents still use workshops to come together to bounce ideas, collaborate and imagine the new. Every one of the human-made objects you can see right now probably came from a creation process that involved workshopping somewhere along the line.

In a short space of time, the workshop has become an essential tool for groups of people to come up with new ideas and solve problems. And yet almost nobody is taught how to run a workshop. The most common approach is to ask people to watch facilitators and 'do what they do'. But watching someone do something doesn't show you even half of what you need to know to do it well. And there are as many styles of facilitation as there are facilitators.

The skills you need to be a great facilitator are teachable and can be learned. We created Curve because we wanted to help organisations build successful teams, come up with great innovations and solve problems. How do we help them achieve these things? We design and run workshops to show how to facilitate their own, so that they carry on the great work themselves.

WHERE ARE WORKSHOPS GOING?

WE started writing this book in 2020, a year like no other. As country after country sent people to 'lockdown' in their homes, collaboration in face-to-face workshops was abandoned, and businesses switched to online platforms like Zoom, Hangouts and Teams. But online workshops weren't new to 2020. We'd already seen the potential of new and cheap technologies and created our Remote Workshop Workshop, training people how to design and run online workshops in a live workshop setting. Our motivation was to cut the carbon emissions of travel but perversely, as the climate emergency became a global uprising, we saw little interest in changing old ways of working. Even workshops co-creating solutions for climate change continued to fly people around the world.

The global lockdown forced the change, when organisations had to 'go remote' and creative work was pushed to individuals or small groups using collaboration tools like Mural and Miro. Often, the interactivity and human connection that defined good in-person workshops was lost, but one of the positive things to come out of the pandemic was the creation of a global petri dish for innovation in remote facilitation, and not just in terms of technology. Visionary facilitators began to incorporate movement, meditation, nature and games into their online workshops. They combined these with tried and tested design-thinking tools to create memorable and enjoyable events. Even sceptics discovered that collaborating remotely can be as good as, or even better than, getting together in a room.

Now more than ever, society and businesses need to solve problems, come up with new ideas and change the way they operate. And with such environmental, financial and accessibility benefits, we really can't afford to go 'back to normal' – we must step boldly into the workshop of the future.

" Together and united, we are unstoppable. "

GRETA THUNBERG

ANYTHING IS POSSIBLE!

VIDEO-CALLING technology has been around for decades, usually for little or no cost, but there's been a reluctance to take full advantage of it. People tell us "it's just not the same as meeting face to face", or "video is fine for regular meetings but not for collaboration", or "we need to get together at least once to build trust".

Don't get us wrong, we've always been fans of what you can achieve when you get people in the same physical space together. But 2020 showed us that when we start to push the boundaries of technology, let go of our assumptions about what is and isn't possible and think creatively about how we can collaborate, the possibilities are infinite.

Today's technology allows us to bring together almost anyone on the planet, whether they're on land or sea or in the air. We can meet in virtual places, record messages, take photos, create drawings and diagrams together, make software and print three-dimensional objects. We can generate ideas and bounce them around the globe to people who can improve them and bring them to fruition.

Together, the capabilities of technology and the effect of a global lockdown have nudged people to do things they hadn't considered possible or didn't want to try. IT departments approved ways of working they'd previously banned. That's a great thought for you to bring into your online workshops – sometimes the idea that something can't work is so entrenched, it takes the necessity brought about by a crisis to show that it can.

Now, as we write this in 2021, we know we can achieve things online that we thought we could only do in person – not only that, we know we can do them even better online. We're at the beginning of a new age of creativity in online collaboration where people all over the world are working together to generate the ideas and solve the problems that will shape our future.

EASIER, BETTER, FASTER, CHEAPER

IF after reading the section above you're still worried about persuading your participants of the benefits of online workshops, here's a handy list you can use to convince the most reluctant:

- No need to spend time, energy and money finding and booking a venue, setting up a room and clearing up afterwards
- Help the planet by cutting the environmental impact of travel
- Remove the cost of travel, venue hire, food and stationery
- Make your workshops more accessible to people with physical disabilities, anxiety or caring responsibilities

- Invite as many people as you like with no added cost
- Adapt and flex your workshop as it unfolds to meet participants' needs
- Message participants and your facilitator team privately
- Transcribe notes, show captions for people speaking and even translate them in real time. Spell-check will make sure every note is correct and legible

Remote workshops are better for your participants too:

- A familiar environment means participants will be more comfortable speaking up
- Anonymous contributions mean they don't need to worry about blame or glory
- No matter how many people are looking at your digital whiteboard, everyone gets the same clear view!
- There's no chance of getting lost trying to find the venue
- People can be fully present in the workshop, without worrying whether they'll be late to pick up the kids because of heavy traffic on the way back from the venue
- Everyone has the same-sized window in the Zoom room, making hierarchy less visible
- No one can sit next to the boss, on their own at the back, or in a clique with their friends

COUNTING THE COST OF CARBON

TO illustrate how remote collaboration can help combat the global climate emergency, we took two online workshops that we ran for clients in 2021 and estimated how much carbon was saved for each one by avoiding air travel. We also estimated the carbon savings made by Curve from avoiding both land and air travel over the course of a year during the pandemic.

We calculated that our client for Workshop One, hosting in New York with eight people attending remotely from the UK, saved approximately 14.5 tonnes CO_2-eq. CO_2-eq is a metric measure used to compare the emissions from various greenhouse gases on the basis of their global-warming potential (GWP), by converting amounts of other gases to the equivalent amount of carbon dioxide with the same GWP.

Workshop Two, a global event with 35 remote attendees from around the world, saved approximately 41.5 tonnes CO_2-eq by hosting this event online.

We only had the data to calculate flight emissions for these two workshops; you can imagine how much more carbon was saved when you factor in land travel, too!

At Curve, the carbon we saved by avoiding all travel and running our workshops online for one year (calculated using UK Government GHG Reporting Conversion Factors for land travel and the carbon calculator at climatecare.org for air travel) stands at more than 100 tonnes CO_2-eq.

So you can see that by running your workshops online, you can play a significant role in addressing the climate crisis. And these impacts are just the tip of the iceberg when you consider all the other environmental costs of travel such as takeaway food and bottled water.

02.

The four pillars of online workshops

All about technology

All about you – the facilitator

All about them – the participants

All about energy

The many elements of an online workshop can ultimately be boiled down to four core pillars. Without a facilitator, participants, and even the most basic technology, the workshop can't happen.

The fourth pillar is just as important though; overlooking energy and how to manage it is the number one reason for an online workshop to fail.

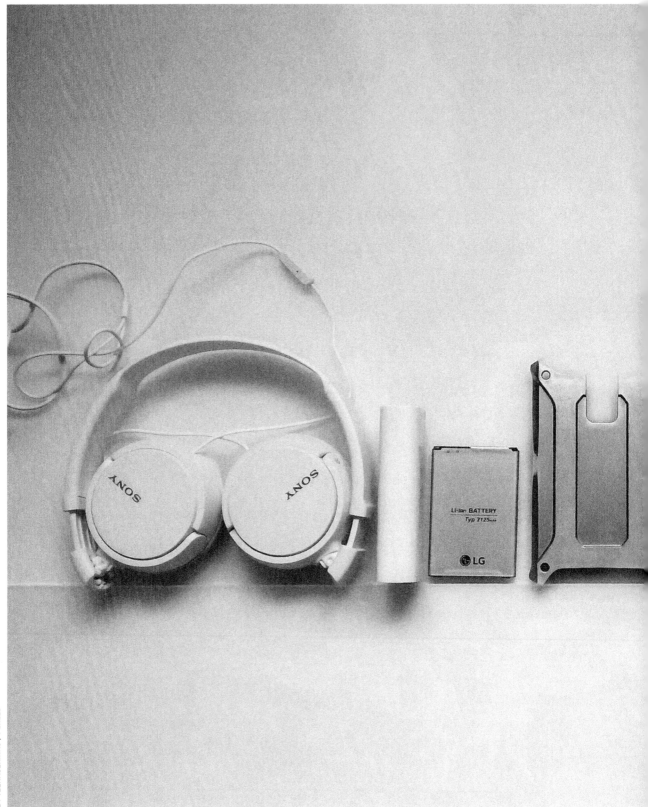

ALL ABOUT TECHNOLOGY

PART 02

MAKE FRIENDS WITH YOUR TECHNOLOGY!

FOR the many people we've trained to run online workshops, their biggest fears are that either the technology will fail, or they will fail at using the technology. We've even seen talented facilitators decline to run online workshops because they find the tech too daunting.

If this is something you're worried about, we're here to show you that you can make friends with the tech and, with a little effort, you can learn to love it and even become famous for how you use it.

In this chapter we'll look at the types of technology you'll need for your workshop and pointers on how to choose it. Because tools are being changed and released almost daily we're only naming a few of the most used here.

ALL ABOUT TECHNOLOGY

PART 02

WHAT TECHNOLOGY DO YOU NEED?

WE'LL talk later about the pitfalls and risks of technology – fear is real, and things can and will go wrong. With preparation, most failures can be avoided. For now, a golden rule that will help you is to keep the tech as simple as you can to meet your goal. The less you use, the less there is to go wrong! This section outlines the different activities you'll need technology for.

Real-time communication

To bring people together in a virtual room, use a video platform like Zoom, Google Hangouts or Microsoft Teams. Voice-only communications on these tools use less bandwidth and data (helpful if people are joining from mobile devices) and make it safe for people to participate if you're setting them tasks to complete while they walk. You can send short text messages within most video platforms and if you want extra functionality you can create groups on other platforms like Slack or WhatsApp.

Sharing content

In some workshops you'll want to share presentations, videos or documents either before or during the session. The simplest

method is to send attachments using email or messaging. You can also share your screen live on most video platforms so that everyone sees the same content at the same time.

Collaborating digitally

The heart of a workshop is the work that participants do together. There are thousands of collaboration platforms, giving you huge flexibility. The simplest are tools like Dropbox, Google Docs or Microsoft OneDrive. For a richer, more visual experience you can use a virtual whiteboard like Mural or Miro, and there are lots of applications designed for specific purposes like project planning or design. You might also need a file-sharing tool like WeTransfer, especially if you're going to be sharing large files such as videos.

Engaging with participants

One of the biggest challenges you'll face in your online workshops is keeping people engaged enough to resist the lure of email and social media notifications. Digital polls, surveys, breakout rooms and playing music are good for keeping everyone focused.

LEARN TO LOVE YOUR TECH!

THE most confident facilitators really do love their technology.
Here's how you can too:

- Pick a core set of tools and use them consistently in all your workshops
- Become an expert in the tools: watch the how-to videos, read the blogs and join the user groups
- Speak to experts and other facilitators to share what you know and learn from them
- Practise, practise, practise!
- Design a fallback plan in case your critical technologies fail

- Do a technical run-through before you start your workshop so you know everything is working
- Be creative! If it's digital you can bring it into your online workshop, so use your imagination.

   You could converse with artificial intelligence or collaborate in TikTok. Incorporate yoga with an instructor in Tibet. Code, buy, swap, sell!

KEEP IT SIMPLE

SINCE the 2020 lockdown forced remote working onto many global knowledge-workers, we've seen digital collaboration tools and video platforms proliferate. Endless video tutorials, webinars and blogs explain how to use them.

This is all good but the focus is usually in the wrong place. These tools are just the digital equivalent of physical spaces and stationery. All this tutorial content is like a university devoted to teaching people how to use meeting rooms, markers and sticky notes.

Keep in mind that ideas are created by people and the way they interact, whether they're in a room together or online. When you choose technology for your remote workshop, ask yourself how it will encourage that interaction for your participants.

INSPRATION:
Find a list of our
favourite technologies.

EXERCISE 2 – CHOOSE YOUR TECH TOOLS

Think about the technologies you're most comfortable with for each of the following categories and write them into the table. If you want inspiration, head over to the Closer Apart website for a list of our favourites.

Real time communication

Sharing content

Collaborating digitally

Engaging with participants

ALL ABOUT YOU – THE FACILITATOR

PART 02

49

THE FACILITATOR JOB DESCRIPTION

A WORKSHOP isn't a workshop without a facilitator! Facilitators can be a member of the workshop group, someone from another part of the organisation, or external to it. The facilitator has six main tasks:

01.
understand the brief and clarify the objectives of the workshop

02.
create a workshop design that maps out a journey leading from the current state to the future objectives

03.
shape the energy levels throughout the workshop and constantly adjust the pace to keep people engaged

04.
make sure every participant is given equal opportunity to contribute

05.

spot conflicting
views and mediate
to help the group
reach agreement

06.

encourage and
support new ideas
and emerging ways
of working

IN short, the facilitator is much like the magician who designs the show, builds the set, performs to delight the audience and finally pulls the rabbit out of the hat. The big difference is that the magician already has the rabbit hidden somewhere, whereas the facilitator gets the participants working together to create their own miraculous rabbit!

So what makes a great facilitator? Is it a certain 'type' of person? Are introverts or extroverts better at the job? Can you be both subject-expert and facilitator in a workshop? Let's have a go at answering these often asked questions.

IS THERE A FACILITATOR 'TYPE'?

LET'S imagine two different people about to run a workshop. Hari's a hedonist. He lives in the moment and loves being surrounded by people enjoying his workshop, smiling and laughing as they work. Dottie thrives on the detail. She loves to see every box ticked and all the outputs completed exactly as specified.

The day before the workshop, both Dottie and Hari find it hard to get to sleep. Dottie's worried she doesn't have all the details written down or that there's something missing from her agenda.

Hari wakes early on the morning of the workshop with a sense of panic; something isn't right. He doesn't really understand how his exercise will work. Is there enough time to get through the work or has he allowed too much? Oh, and did he remember to invite people?

On the day, Dottie fusses with printouts, worried about what might go wrong. She comes across as anxious and irritable. Her participants find it hard to relax and feel they're being judged, making it hard to fully engage in the workshop.

Meanwhile, over in Hari's workshop, the participants are confused: there's been a delay at the start and uncomfortable pauses throughout the first session as he tries to work out what he's doing. There's a slight sense of panic as Hari looks for missing materials and tries to sort out the tech he hasn't set up properly. Hari cracks jokes to keep everyone smiling, but they're starting to feel like this is a waste of time.

If their workshops somehow turn out to be a success, Dottie is delighted because everything went exactly to her plan and nothing unexpected happened. Hari is happy because although the unexpected did happen, he was able to guide the group seamlessly to a breakthrough on a wing and a prayer.

WHERE ARE YOU ON THE HARI-DOTTIE SPECTRUM?

DID you notice something of yourself, or of facilitators you know, in Hari or Dottie? They're extreme character types, but they exist to some extent in all of us. Approaches to planning often align with the facilitator's specific mindset and where on the 'Hari-Dottie' spectrum they lie.

If you're like Hari, you probably avoid detailed plans. You rely on your ability to sense the mood in the room and you improvise accordingly. You're excellent at making things up on the fly and you look confident in difficult situations. You tell people you're good at 'winging it'.

If you're more like Dottie, the planning phase is where you're in your element. You love to break the workshop down into its smallest components, and in your plan every minute is counted, every activity is scripted and every output is described. You're excellent at anticipating challenges and imagining 'what if' scenarios.

In reality an ideal facilitator sits somewhere between these two, balancing preparation and attention to detail with a can-do attitude and an improvisational spirit.

INTROVERTS AND EXTROVERTS

BRING Hari and Dottie to mind. It turns out Dottie is quite an introvert. She finds the workshop experience quite draining. Being around lots of different people is exhausting and she usually recharges by finding quiet time alone. And Hari? You've guessed it, he happens to be an extrovert. He feeds on the energy of other people and loves the fast pace and high energy of the workshop experience. Hari's at home in a crowd and when he wants to recharge, he likes to socialise with friends.

This is a great way to think about introverts and extroverts as facilitators:
INTROVERTED: Big Eyes, Big Ears
EXTROVERTED: Big Hands, Big Mouth

HARI and Dottie are brilliant facilitators in different ways. Here's what makes them so good and how each makes the most of their particular talent. As you can imagine, when they facilitate together the workshop runs like a dream.

	DOTTIE THE INTROVERT	HARI THE EXTROVERT
STRENGTHS	■ Excellent at reading the room ■ High levels of empathy ■ Great listener	■ Able to inject high levels of energy ■ Motivates people to action ■ Senses and shapes the dynamics between people
GET THE BEST FROM THEM WHEN THEY...	■ Offer to lead emotionally charged sessions ■ Take time for themself before, during and after the workshop ■ Connect one on one with challenging participants	■ Offer to lead in low-energy slots (e.g. after lunch) ■ Get on with follow-up tasks immediately after the workshops - they'll be on a roll ■ Focus on acknowledging quieter participants
REMOTE SUPERPOWER	■ Comfortable 'speaking to the void' – a screen filled with faces giving very little feedback!	■ Can engage and enthuse participants when the energy dips

Of course this is much more complex than a simple binary. We all exist on a spectrum of introversion to extroversion.

EXERCISE 3 – YOU AS A FACILITATOR

Where do you think you are on the spectrum as a facilitator?

What tip will you keep in mind for your next workshop?

SPOTLIGHT ON

Artist and Cultural Geographer
HOLLEY M. KHOLI-MURCHISON

Talking about
TELLING YOUR STORY

USE YOUR BODY

HUMAN beings are highly attuned to body language. We pick up signals from each other's posture and facial expressions. When we're looking at screens in remote workshops it's easy to forget this hardwiring in our brains is still at work. When you're facilitating, use your face and your body to communicate, as well as your voice. Make sure you have a comfortable seat and you can move your arms freely. Bring your hands into view whenever you can to emphasise points, and keep a smile on your face.

CO-FACILITATION

IN our experience, workshops are always more successful when you facilitate as a pair. One can give instructions and lead exercises while the other pays attention to the facial expressions and body language of participants, ready to step in if anyone's struggling. While you're speaking, your co-facilitator can prepare for the next exercises, arrange breakout groups, create online polls, welcome latecomers, troubleshoot technology or simply tidy up the shared workspace. They can answer questions and solve problems in the chat and spot if anyone drops off the session. If your sponsor wants to change the direction of the workshop while it's in progress, they can meet with your co-facilitator to agree the new design.

Your co-facilitator can also monitor your energy level and intervene if they see you're flagging. You might be tempted to push on through, but it's hard to maintain the group's energy or pay close attention to conversations if you're running close to empty.

For online workshops, it's essential to have one facilitator looking after the technology and another running the

exercises – trying to do both is stressful for you and won't work for your participants. Both co-facilitators should be able to lead all parts of the agenda, even though you have an initial plan that splits out the responsibilities. Co-facilitation will give your participants a much better experience. Listening to one voice for long periods of time can get monotonous, especially online. Switching between speakers adds variety and lifts the energy. Participants will find it easier to concentrate and retain information, and will rate your workshop more highly!

For larger groups, it's worth dedicating a third person to the technology with no facilitation role. For us, the cut-off point comes where you can't see your whole group on one screen – about twenty people, depending on your video platform.

Of course it's not always possible to have a co-facilitator. There simply might not be enough budget or anyone available, but remember how much more powerful it can be and try to convince others to invest in co-facilitation if you can.

"

I never scored a goal in my life without getting a pass from someone else.

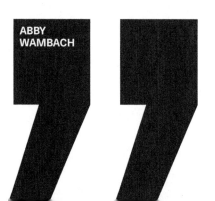

ABBY WAMBACH

"

WHO DO YOU NEED AS
YOUR CO-FACILITATOR?

WHEN you're thinking about potential co-facilitators, consider your respective skills, styles and energy. Find someone who's good at the tasks you find more difficult and who enjoys the things you don't. If you're really into the big picture then look for someone who loves the detail or vice versa. The best facilitation pairs complement each other. It can also be useful to partner with someone who's an expert in the subject matter you're discussing or the technology you're using.

FACILITATOR TIP:
Rehearse your workshop end to end with your co-facilitator or team in advance to make sure you're completely comfortable with the technology you'll be using.

THE ANATOMY OF A FACILITATOR

THIS is where we start to look at the qualities, skills and beliefs that will make you a successful facilitator. You might discover areas where you want to build on your skills or develop your talents. Remember your growth mindset; there's nothing here you couldn't do... you just haven't done it yet.

QUALITIES	SKILLS	BELIEFS
A great facilitator is	**A great facilitator can**	**A great facilitator believes**
Observant	Synthesise information	All people have contributions
Challenging	Manage time	to make
Curious	Emphasise facial and body language	All people come with
Neutral	Create a safe space	positive intent
Adaptable	Model behaviour	If the problem is in the room,
Comfortable with silence	Keep track of time	the solution is in the room
Patient	Clarify, synthesise and summarise	The facilitator doesn't need to
Approachable	Communicate clearly	be the expert
Engaging	Inspire people	In the power of the growth mindset
Energetic	Bring in personal experience	
Diplomatic	Join dots in conversations	
Inclusive	Apply creative problem-solving	
Humorous	Prepare to the nth degree	
Calm	Organise	
Empathetic		
Firm		
Fun!		

EXERCISE 4 – WHAT MAKES A GREAT FACILITATOR?

We asked you earlier to think about a really great workshop – do you remember the person or people who led it? Take a moment to think about the attributes that make a really great facilitator. What qualities do they have? What skills? Jot your notes around the 'anatomy of a facilitator' illustration below.

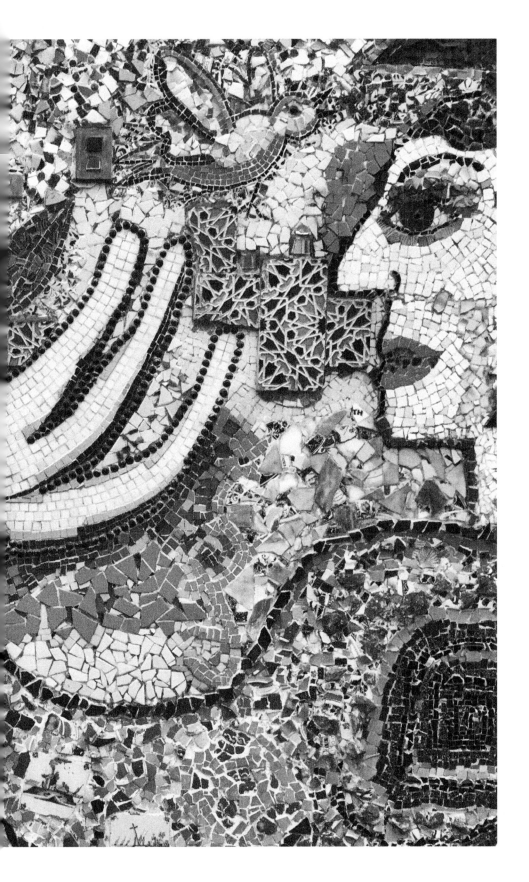

ALL ABOUT THEM – THE PARTICIPANTS

Brilliant remote workshops are all about people. For the hundreds of facilitators we've trained, their number one need is to learn how to deal with people, especially the challenging ones.

This shouldn't be a surprise – after all, the purpose of the workshop is to harness the collective wisdom of the people there.

WE'RE ALL HUMAN

A GREAT place to start when thinking about your participants is that essentially, we're all the same – we're human beings. We all need to eat, breathe, sleep and, crucially, we all strive to find meaning through what we do. We've found that when you guide people to work together and really give the best of themselves to create something new, your workshop can create opportunities for self-discovery, growth and a deep sense of personal satisfaction for both you and your participants.

Another useful perspective to keep in mind when thinking about your participants is 'API,' an acronym given to us by a wonderful client at the United Nations University. Commonly used in computing, the client re-tooled the letters to stand for 'Assume Positive Intent.' No matter how disruptive or problematic a participant might seem in the moment, the likelihood is they're driven by good intentions.

WHAT TYPE OF COLLABORATION DO YOU NEED?

COLLABORATION is one of those words that's used an awful lot and yet it's hard to pin down exactly what it means, partly because it's used to describe different activities. In 2015 we conducted research with academics from Cambridge University and University College London into what makes for great collaboration. The results showed that there are different types of collaboration that need different conditions to succeed, depending on the outcome you're trying to achieve. Our research identified the following three forms of collaboration:

COLLABORATE TO CREATE

This most commonly happens in workshops where people are getting together to come up with something brand new. For it to succeed, people need to welcome and build on each other's ideas. Time and space is another important condition for success, and visual inspiration really helps the process.

Use ideation exercises to come up with new concepts – a quick web search will give you hundreds to choose from. Improving and building on ideas is also critical. Use our simple three-question feedback framework to help your participants give effective feedback:

CURVE FEEDBACK FRAMEWORK

When asking for feedback on any idea or piece of work, ask these three questions:

1. **What did you like?**
2. **What would you like more of?**
3. **What questions do you still have?**

COLLABORATE TO CONTROL

In this form of collaboration you're
looking to create repeatable or
high-quality outputs, or to control the
way that something is done to make sure
it's consistent. Workshops that use this
form of collaboration are often trying to
perfect processes or embed new ways
of working or behaviour. The energy of
the workshop needs to be calm and focused
and you'll need to assign someone the role
of quality checker.

COLLABORATE TO COMPETE

In this scenario the purpose of collaboration
is to come up with the greatest quantity
of outputs or to deliver at the fastest pace.
You might be creating a proposal to a tight
deadline, or a large amount of code or
documentation. You want a very high
level of energy here, and you probably
want to encourage a competitive mindset.
It's critical to have someone responsible
for timekeeping, who can also act as
a cheerleader!

EXERCISE 5 – YOUR COLLABORATION TYPE

We've seen that each collaboration archetype needs different energy levels, people and tools. Is the purpose of your workshop to create, compete or control?

How will this shape who you invite and the tools and exercises you use?

WHO SHOULD BE AT YOUR WORKSHOP?

WHEN you plan your workshop, think about the outcome and outputs you're aiming for. Who needs to be at the workshop in order to achieve these goals? Choosing who to invite is critical. There's a simple and effective management tool we like to use that will help you with this process; it's called RACI, which stands for Responsible, Accountable, Consulted, Informed. You can also use it as the basis of an exercise to assign people to tasks in project or roadmap planning during the workshop.

RESPONSIBLE: These people are going to be doing the hard grind in the workshop – they need to be there. If it's a small team you're working with, you could invite everyone. If it's a larger organisation, invite a diverse and representative subset.

ACCOUNTABLE: This person or group is your most important stakeholder. They decide what actions to take based on the results of the workshop. Having them in the workshop will save time as they can give guidance or make decisions about budgets on the spot, but watch out for power dynamics; sometimes senior people can skew the conversation or inhibit others from contributing.

FACILITATOR TIP:

At the start of the workshop it's great if senior people can encourage other participants to contribute. Brief them in advance to do this. Encourage these senior people to model sharing talk-time. Getting them on your side in this way will instantly change the dynamic in the workshop.

C

I

CONSULTED: Think about who you need to bring in to supply useful information – users of your product or service? Customers? Experts? It's also a good idea to invite people who can champion the output of your workshop – if they're involved they'll naturally be more supportive. Remember to think about energy too. Are there people who could bring some fun to a serious group, or create calm in a frenetic one?

INFORMED: People who only need to know the outcome of your workshop don't need to be there at the session. You can bring them up to speed afterwards, the easiest way being a presentation. Include information on the process – how you got to where you did – and ask a respected participant from the workshop to help you tell the story. One of the most engaging ways to share the outcome is to show a video of the work in progress, including short interviews with participants. Make a plan to do this in advance. Once the workshop is over you can't get it back, but hitting the record button on Zoom or taking some footage on your phone is super simple and gives you raw material to work with later.

A DIVERSE GROUP
GETS BETTER OUTCOMES

ONE of the positive developments of recent times has been a much greater focus on diversity, especially in terms of race, gender, sexuality and background.

Inviting a diverse group of people to your workshop not only promotes fairness and equality, it leads to better outcomes. Great ideas come from a combination of different perspectives. If you don't have those perspectives in your session, the work you create just won't be as interesting or effective. Raising this conversation with clients can feel awkward, but by doing so you'll start to get others thinking, and support the changes needed for fairer, more equal workplaces.

One of the huge advantages of online workshops is that you can really push the boundaries of inclusion and accessibility. It's easier to include people with disabilities, those who can't or don't want to travel, and people who want to remain anonymous.

All behaviour is communication. A few minutes of listening, observing and understanding, can save hours of miscommunication, frustration and conflict. A need met is a problem solved.

L.R. KNOST

MANAGING CHALLENGING BEHAVIOUR

REMEMBER when we said that dealing with people was the most common objective for people on our facilitation training programmes? The vast majority said their specific objective was how to deal with 'difficult people' or 'bad participants.'

At Curve we don't use the terms 'bad' or 'difficult' for people; we firmly believe that all behaviour is simply a form of communication. It's our job as facilitators to work out what that communication is telling us. We use the term 'challenging behaviour'. Think of the behaviour you see as an expression of an unmet need. Thinking about it this way changes the way you relate to it. Rather than a challenge to you as facilitator or an attack on you as an individual, see it instead as a puzzle to work out and potentially even a gift for you to use. When you uncover the unmet needs behind a behaviour, you might be surprised. Here's an example to illustrate the point.

Lizzie here. In a workshop for a large global bank, our senior client and sponsor became very aggressive towards me during an exercise where I was asking participants to write ideas on paper and take photos to send in. I was surprised by this behaviour because the workshop was there to meet her objectives and yet she challenged the exercise and undermined my authority as facilitator. My solution was to call a quick break and have a conversation with her in a breakout room. I told her I noticed the exercise didn't seem to be working for her and asked what she needed. It turned out she was dyslexic and didn't want to write in front of her colleagues, who didn't know. I changed the exercise format so that participants called out ideas and I wrote them on a shared document. With this very simple change, our client was transformed back into our biggest supporter.

We have lots of similar examples, all with different but often very simple solutions that can turn behaviour around in an instant. You might find yourself tempted to push on and ignore challenging behaviour or worse, to call it out and potentially cause shame. Try to pay attention to challenging behaviour in your workshops and avoid public shaming at all costs. Ask yourself, "What is this behaviour telling me? What is the unmet need and how can I meet it?" The easiest way is to just ask.

The diversity and different experiences of your participants means there's potential for all sorts of needs, with a corresponding range of challenging behaviours for you to manage. The image opposite shows a spectrum of common needs, ranging from the most passive to the most dominant. Discovering the unmet needs gives you a shortcut to the action you need to take to change the behaviour. Even if you don't have the time to uncover the need, there are many techniques you can use to stop participants from disrupting the session. These fall into three broad categories:

FACILITATOR TIP:
Here's a simple phrase to use – give it a go.
You'll be pleasantly surprised!
"I notice that...
[state what you notice, with no judgement].
What do you need to make this work for you?"

PART 02

CHANGE THE FORM

The form of a workshop exercise refers to the way you arrange people to complete a task – usually in pairs, or in small or large groups. Don't let participants or even sponsors know this level of detail in advance of a workshop – that way you can change it without anyone noticing. Changing the form is the easiest and most effective way to shift the dynamics of a workshop. If a group is struggling in pairs, combine the pairs into groups of four to introduce more energy and ideas. Conversely if you've got one or two people dominating the conversation in a large group, create breakout rooms and put people into pairs. It's harder to dominate in a conversation with just one other person, so the behaviour changes instantly.

CHANGE THE EXERCISE

For the most important exercises it's worth preparing more than one approach for achieving the goal. This takes more preparation than changing the form as you might need different tools or instructions. For example, if you're trying to create a vision for a team but the participants keep getting stuck on tiny details of language, try switching them to using images rather than text and encourage them to think metaphorically. You can capture language from the conversation around the images and arrive at the vision through this different route. Be creative in the way you modify exercises by introducing techniques like role-play, drawing, mime or even singing. The options are endless so run free with your imagination.

INTERVENE DIRECTLY

This is the most obvious way to change behaviour. Different facilitators have different personal styles, and some are comfortable being very direct with participants. At Curve we believe it's best to avoid confrontation with participants, especially in front of the group. The negative effect is more pronounced in remote workshops as the person speaking is highlighted on the screen. Try calling short breaks and asking participants to get a drink while you have a one-to-one conversation with the person or people behaving in a challenging way. Work out what their unmet need is and adapt what you're doing accordingly. In most cases you'll be able to get the workshop back on track before the others are back with their tea.

EXERCISE 6 – WHO DO YOU NEED AT YOUR WORKSHOP?

Using the RACI grid provided, identify the participants you need for your workshop.

R

RESPONSIBLE: who is going to be responsible for taking things forward?

A

ACCOUNTABLE: who is ultimately on the hook for success?

C

CONSULTED: who do you need to consult for input or feedback?

I

INFORMED: who needs to know about what you've achieved?

ALL ABOUT ENERGY

PART 02

Ever had days when completing the most simple task is a challenge? The feeling of being 'stuck'? Compare it with the days when you power through your to-do list with ease, completely unaware of time.

Creative people often describe this high-quality energy as 'flow', the mental state of being completely present and fully immersed in a task.

HOW TO MOVE FROM 'STUCK' TO 'FLOW'

IT'S all about energy! When energy is high in a workshop, the results can be truly magical. People work faster and smarter, and the combined effect of this momentum and the mental sparks it creates are exponential. We've seen workshop teams create in minutes what would take many weeks back at their desks.

Excitement and fatigue are contagious. Imagine being part of a group watching a nail-biting match or waiting for a band to come on stage, and contrast that feeling with the moment you see a wave of yawns start to travel around a room. As facilitator, you're in a position to understand, shape and manage the energy of the group.

Everything you do depends on your energy levels, and these are influenced by food and drink, rest and exercise. Participants are human beings, and, like you, they're subject to natural rhythms of energy that rise and fall throughout the day. These changes follow a pattern. Once you understand the pattern you can work with it to get your workshop to a state of flow and keep it there for longer.

The diagram opposite will help you understand how energy levels change throughout the day. Remember, energy doesn't just affect participants, it affects you!

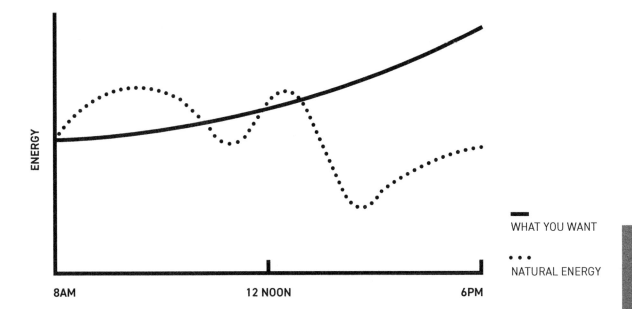

ENERGY

8AM   12 NOON   6PM

—— WHAT YOU WANT

• • • NATURAL ENERGY

THE dotted line shows how energy changes through the day if left to its own devices. People enter the workshop after a good night's sleep and some breakfast. They may well have had caffeine and in the morning their energy level will be relatively high. As the workshop gets going their energy rises as they encounter new people and concepts. Energy dips after a period of working, but as lunchtime approaches it rises in anticipation of food and drink. The effects of nutrition last for a while but as the body starts to redirect its energy to the stomach to digest food, energy levels drop dramatically during what's often referred to as 'the graveyard shift'. Unfortunately, this is often the point at which you ask your participants to do the hardest work. Energy levels rise to hit a peak halfway through the afternoon before drifting down again towards the end of the day.

The solid line shows the target energy level you want to achieve. Note how it rises gently over the course of the workshop to finish at the highest point, with no extreme peaks or troughs along the way.

YOU have many tools at your disposal to manage energy in an online workshop, falling into three categories:

PACING EXERCISES

When you're planning your workshop, think about the point on the energy curve where every exercise falls. If you plan an exercise for a time when energy is naturally high, you can afford to take more time and run more complex exercises. If you expect energy levels to be lower at that point, keep exercises short or break them up. Can different parts of the exercise be completed in different ways? Introducing variety will raise energy levels and help your participants stay engaged.

USE VISUAL INFORMATION

As we mentioned earlier in the book, information presented visually is retained better. It's more interesting to look at and more powerful. The brain processes images thousands of times faster than written language. Giving information in visual form is especially useful if some of your participants aren't working in their first language – they won't need to spend time and energy translating so many words in their heads.

NUTRITION

What you eat and drink has a direct impact on your energy level. Remind everyone of this fact and suggest snacks to have on hand during the workshop. Try to avoid peaks and troughs by suggesting everyone eat a balanced meal including complex carbohydrates beforehand, with highly nutritious snacks like nuts and raw vegetables on hand during the workshop. Explain that these foods are harder for the body to break down, giving them a slow release of energy to aid focus over long periods. Find a nutrition guide for online workshops on the Closer Apart website.

NUTRITION GUIDE: Look at our Workshop Nutrition Guide here.

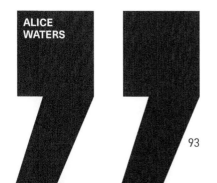

How we eat can change the world.

ALICE
WATERS

ENERGISERS

The most direct way to change the energy level in your workshop is to introduce exercises we call energisers. Unrelated to the workshop subject matter, their goal is purely to change how people feel through physical movement. If they can, ask participants to go outside. Even a few minutes of daylight can dramatically affect mood and energy. When people spend hours working on computers, especially laptops, shoulders become tense and sore, brows furrow and eyestrain causes headaches. People often resist energiser activities, describing them as awkward or silly and claiming they don't have time. Explain how these energisers improve the quality and quantity of the work you're doing together. Try to include some form of energiser in every workshop segment.

FACILITATOR TIP:
If you're really pressed for time but you sense the energy in the group is low, try this: Ask people to sit up straight, roll their shoulders back, focus their eyes on the furthest thing they can see out of a window and take three big deep breaths. This will reset muscles, rest the eyes, loosen the posture and refocus the mind – all in just 30 seconds!

WE'LL talk more about energisers in the chapter on 'Middles' but for now just think back to those scenarios of 'stuck' and 'flow' at the start of the chapter. Your goal is to help your participants stay in 'flow' for as much time as possible – with steady, high levels of energy so that they can do their very best work.

EXERCISE: JUMPING 8S
Let's give it a go:
1. Pause for a moment. Close your eyes and rate your energy level on a scale of 1-10 where 1 is low and 10 is high.
2: Put this book down, and stand where you have space to move.
3: Do 8 star jumps!
4: Sit back down, close your eyes and note how your energy has changed.

03.

Making the magic happen

The steps involved in preparing, designing and running your workshop are many, and can seem daunting. We'll show you what you need to do and when, how to avoid the pitfalls, and how to make sure your workshops don't get derailed by the unexpected.

Use this section whenever you run a workshop so that you can deliver the magic every time.

MEETING, PRESENTATION OR WORKSHOP?

MEETING, PRESENTATION OR WORKSHOP?

ONE of the reasons we wrote this book is because we've heard so many people say, "I hate workshops!" and, even worse, "workshops online don't really work". It's so frustrating to hear this when we know that a well-designed workshop in the hands of a great facilitator will have the very opposite effect. So why do so many people have such a strong aversion? When we dig a little deeper, it usually turns out these 'workshops' people hate so much aren't in fact workshops at all, but badly run meetings or presentations!

The most common expectation mismatch is over workshops versus presentations. We ask everyone who comes to our facilitation workshops what they dislike about workshops and the number one response is "too many slides". That's a clear giveaway that what they were attending was a presentation and not a workshop. We should say here that presentations don't have to be long and boring with "too many slides", but that's for another book.

Let's be clear about the definitions, then. In one sense, presentations, meetings and workshops all come under the umbrella term 'meeting' as they all conform to its dictionary definition of 'when two or more people come together to discuss something'. We prefer to use three distinct definitions to avoid any confusion and to make sure everyone understands what we mean by 'workshop':

MEETING

When people use the term 'meeting' at work, what they often mean is a gathering where people get together to share information and make decisions. These are typically regular project meetings, team meetings or daily stand-up meetings. Because these meetings exist within the hierarchy of an organisation or project, there's usually a decision maker. Meetings like these can be informal and last a few minutes, or they can last for hours, entail careful planning and produce lots of documentation such as agendas, action lists and minutes.

PRESENTATION

This is a meeting where a group (often large) is brought together to receive information, usually from one or two presenters who are experts in their subject matter. The content in a presentation is usually fixed and they can be delivered repeatedly. Interactivity is often limited to a question and answer session at the end. The best presentations are well-rehearsed and dynamically delivered, holding the listener's attention and taking them on an emotional journey.

WHEN we ask people to describe a
meeting or a presentation, most come
up with something close to the definitions
on the previous page. Ask them to define
a workshop and there's a fair bit of
head-scratching and some pretty varied
interpretations! We've evolved our own
definition at Curve, which our facilitators
find helpful when they're proposing
workshops or persuading people to attend:

A workshop is a group of people working together, engaged in activity to learn, to create and to change.

JOHN
MONKS &
LIZZIE
SHUPAK

EVERY word in the definition is important,
so let's expand on them a little:

GROUP

A workshop is typically attended by between 4 and 20 people.

ENGAGED

Everyone is actively participating.

ACTIVITY

Work gets done.

LEARN

Knowledge is passed on.

CREATE

New ideas, products or systems are developed.

CHANGE

The world is moved forward.

A NOTE ON TRAINING:

One of the most important reasons people meet is to pass on knowledge –
to teach and to learn. Any of the meeting types can be used for training,
but workshops are an especially good format for learning because of the
group participation and engagement.

THE last three words in the definition neatly describe the three core reasons to run a workshop:

1. to come up with new ideas and solutions to problems (to create)
2. to get people aligned and excited about doing something differently (to change)
3. to help participants understand, engage with and practise new skills (to learn)

You'll often find that your workshop involves elements of more than one of the above. If you're facilitating a team to come up with a new vision and values for the company (create), you'll also want to generate buy-in to those values among the team (change).

MIX & MATCH

IT'S perfectly ok to run more than one meeting type in sequence – in fact, it's often a great idea to have a presentation at the start of a workshop so that everybody starts with the same level of knowledge. Equally it's sometimes useful to hold a more formal meeting after a workshop to make decisions and assign actions. What's critical is that you make it clear to your participants what type of meeting they're coming to. If you're presenting at the start of a workshop, make it clear when the presentation ends: stop showing slides and simply say, "presentation over".

Use the table opposite to make sure you're planning for the right purpose, and that what you plan will meet the expectations of your participants.

	MEETING	PRESENTATION	WORKSHOP
PURPOSE	■ Share information ■ Provide updates ■ Allocate tasks ■ Have a discussion ■ Make decisions	■ Communicate static information from one to many	■ Develop new ideas ■ Learn by sharing experiences ■ Motivate and align people ■ Create change
SIZE	■ Ideally 5-20 but an expertly chaired meeting can manage hundreds (e.g. parliament)	■ Limited only by technology – in theory all the roughly 5 billion people with an internet connected device could watch the same presentation	■ Ideally 15-20 participants per pair of facilitators. ■ Workshops can be much larger with more facilitators – we've run workshops for hundreds of people at a time
PEOPLE	■ Chairperson ■ Attendees	■ Presenter or presenters ■ Audience	■ Facilitator or facilitators ■ Participants
REMOTE FORMAT	■ Video meeting ■ Conference call	■ Presentation decks ■ Webinar ■ Video meeting with presenter-view ■ Can be live or recorded	■ Video platform with multiple 'rooms' for group work
IN-PERSON FORMAT	■ Stand-up ■ Seated round a conference table	■ Front of meeting room ■ Conference stage ■ Can be live or recorded	■ Large open meeting spaces so people can move around ■ Plenty of light, wall space and few tables
ADDITIONAL REMOTE TOOLS	■ Shared documents ■ Voting tools	■ Polling apps ■ Interactive Q&A	■ Remote visual collaboration tools (eg Mural, Miro). ■ Specific tools for the work you're trying to create

PLANNING YOUR WORKSHOP

PART 03

WORKSHOPS ARE EXPERIENCES

HAVE you ever been to Disneyland? Even if you haven't you can probably imagine the experience. The magic of the famous films is woven through every moment – the advertising, the booking process, entering the park, eating and drinking, the rides and even the queues. Nothing is accidental, everything is carefully planned to influence the way you think, feel and act. Whatever you feel about Disney's aim to get people to buy more plastic princesses, it's certainly a masterclass in experience design.

Think of your workshop in the same way. You're designing an experience: your goal is to get your participants to think, feel and act a certain way at every moment, from their first invitation, through every exercise, to their five-star review on your feedback form.

"

Never be limited by other people's limited imaginations.

DR MAE JEMISON

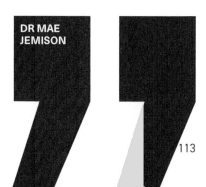

THE REMOTE WORKSHOP
PLANNING CANVAS

WE created our Remote Workshop Planning Canvas to help you design brilliant workshops. It works for a single workshop or for a longer programme of sessions. You can use it to guide the conversation as you take a workshop brief and turn it into a high-level design. You'll find a template and an instruction video on how to use the canvas, as well as an interactive version, on the Closer Apart website. Have it in front of you before you read the rest of this section.

The canvas will help you to think through all the elements you need for a workshop that delivers not just its objectives, but a really memorable experience for your participants. And it'll help you avoid the most common pitfalls in workshop planning.

SECTION 1 captures all the information you need to start designing. We like to think of it as our 'workshop brief on a page', covering the background context, work already done, what success looks like, what your workshop needs to produce and, most importantly, who's coming and how they'll be thinking, feeling and behaving when they arrive.

SECTION 2 captures risks, materials and technology requirements. Armed with this information, you're ready to create the optimum design.

SECTION 3 of the canvas guides you through creating your workshop's flow and activities. It's broken into two complementary parts. The Workshop Overview maps out the journey of your workshop. What are the topics or focus areas you want to cover? Use the set of prompt words shown below to provoke your thinking and change these if you want to alter the tone of the workshop based on the top half of the canvas. For example, if your group is already comfortable with each other and you want to inject energy and new ideas, you might change DISARM to INSPIRE.

SECTION 4 is for Workshop Activities. This comes last on purpose so don't be tempted to jump straight to it; you should only select your activities once you've looked at the requirements, the people and the workshop overview together.

 PLANNING CANVAS:
Scan the QR code to download your own planning canvas

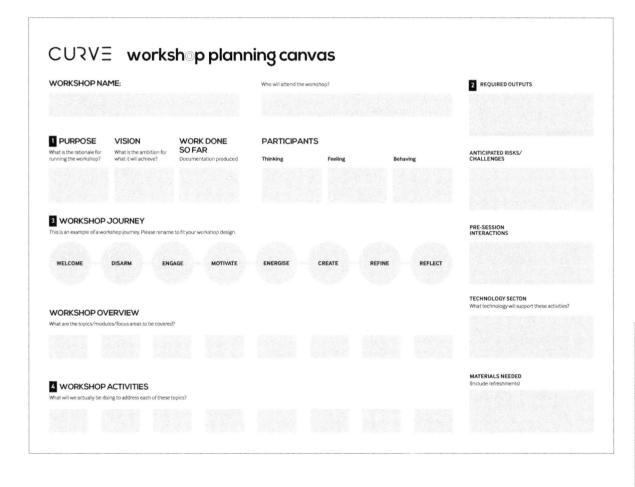

CURVE workshop planning canvas

WORKSHOP NAME:

Who will attend the workshop?

2 REQUIRED OUTPUTS

1 PURPOSE

VISION

WORK DONE SO FAR

What is the rationale for running the workshop?

What is the ambition for what it will achieve?

Documentation produced

PARTICIPANTS

Thinking · Feeling · Behaving

ANTICIPATED RISKS/ CHALLENGES

3 WORKSHOP JOURNEY

This is an example of a workshop journey. Please rename to fit your workshop design.

WELCOME · DISARM · ENGAGE · MOTIVATE · ENERGISE · CREATE · REFINE · REFLECT

PRE-SESSION INTERACTIONS

TECHNOLOGY SECTON

What technology will support these activities?

WORKSHOP OVERVIEW

What are the topics/modules/focus areas to be covered?

4 WORKSHOP ACTIVITIES

What will we actually be doing to address each of these topics?

MATERIALS NEEDED

(Include refreshments)

CONSIDER OUTCOMES FIRST

WHEN planning your workshop it's tempting to start by thinking about the exercises you have in mind. A better place to start is the outcome you want to achieve. Include tangible outputs such as 'we want to define a vision for our new team', as well as more emotion-based goals such as 'we want people to understand the opportunity', or 'we want an excited and motivated team'.

HOW TO GET THE PERFECT BRIEF

WALK through the workshop planning canvas with the person commissioning the workshop or, if you're doing it for yourself, put the kettle on and spend a few minutes using the canvas to organise your thoughts. At this stage you've got a great basis for your plan. This is the point in the process where we always ask our clients a single powerful question:

"If you could only choose one thing you want from this workshop, what would it be?"

Whether you're asking a client or asking yourself, this question will flush out the key priority for the workshop.

You'll find the answer often differs from the initially stated workshop purpose. We know that workshops have both outputs (tangible) and outcomes (changes in human behaviour and attitudes). People usually describe an output ('a plan for...' 'a design of...') when asked to state their objective for the workshop but when asked "what one thing...?" they'll describe an outcome like 'motivation', 'alignment' or 'buy-in'.

WHAT'S ALREADY BEEN DONE?

A COMMON pitfall, especially when you're external to the working group, is missing context and background for the session you're about to run. Sometimes this won't matter too much, as a great workshop experience can uncover new perspectives on old questions. But sometimes, the criticism of, "we've already done this", can completely derail the journey and leave you at a loss.

As you're talking to your workshop clients, ask them what work has already been done on the topic. Have there been previous meetings or workshops? Has documentation already been created? The more you know the better.

FACILITATOR TIP:
"We've tried this before and it didn't work" is one of the most frequent protests of people resistant to change. This shouldn't be a reason not to try again. Instead, frame your response as, "how do we learn from that experience in order to make this attempt successful?"

AVOIDING THE BUMPS IN THE ROAD

EVERY workshop has risks, from technical and practical to personal and emotional. The more you've anticipated these risks and put plans in place to manage them, the easier it will be to make your workshop run smoothly and stay calm.

TECHNOLOGY: LESS IS MORE

The first risk category to address is technology. To repeat our Curve mantra on technology, use the minimum amount of tech to get the job done. Try to avoid the tendency, especially common in innovation-focused environments, to get carried away with shiny new software and collaboration tools.

Even the best technologies are susceptible to failure from the most trivial causes. A leader of a global tech giant dropped out of one of our recent workshops because their child unplugged their Wi-Fi router. And even if you've protected against that risk, there are many more ways your participants' tech can fail: Wi-Fi drops out, devices overheat, internet connections become unstable, batteries die, mobile coverage fades, software subscriptions expire and computers decide to update their software at a critical moment.

You can't control most of these events, but there are three things you can do to minimise the risks:

- Reduce the number of technologies you're using in your workshop
- Give your participants tips on how to prepare their tech (make sure your devices are charged, update your software, test your internet connection and move if necessary)
- Have a 'plan B' for if critical technology fails. A top tip here is to make sure that everyone has a pen and paper handy when they join. You can reproduce almost any collaboration tool by getting people to write or draw on their notepads and send photos using their phones

BE PREPARED FOR SABOTEURS

The second big risk category is people. For our workshops we make sure we're pre-warned about people likely to display challenging behaviour by asking the right questions in advance. The next biggest worry for most facilitators is people who just won't engage.

Keep in mind that 'forewarned is forearmed'. The more you know about your attendees the better.

DON'T FORGET THE REFRESHMENTS!

In the physical world, even the most poorly equipped workshop rooms will have water available, and many will have teas, coffees and snacks. There's a tendency to forget that when people join workshops remotely, they still need sustenance. You can take care of this very simply by sending an email suggesting people have water and some healthy snacks to hand. Even better, send goodies through the mail so that your workshop participants can eat and drink together. Sharing food is an age-old element of human connection and will help your participants feel closer together even though they're apart.

FACILITATOR TIP:

We ran a remote workshop with people attending from America, Europe and Australia. Beforehand, we sent everybody a package containing a notepad, pen and special teas. Half way through the workshop we all made tea together and performed our own version of a Chinese tea ceremony. Drinking tea together in a peaceful and calm way created a special kind of positive energy and created a bond between attendees.

SPLITTING OUT THE GROUP

Many video-conferencing platforms let you assign participants to breakout rooms. Dividing the group up is a great way to increase the energy, get more work done and allow parallel streams of activity to happen at the same time. In general, breakout groups that don't have a facilitator work best with three to six people. You can also use the breakout rooms to create pairs and encourage deeper conversations.

If your video platform doesn't support breakout rooms, a workaround is to create multiple simultaneous meetings and share links to them at the appropriate point in the workshop. You'll lose some of the functionality like the ability to broadcast messages or use a common chat, and you can't use the technology to force people back to the main session. Give clear instructions telling people what time to return to the main meeting, and leave yourself a bit more time around exercises. Despite the drawbacks, this approach of multiple meetings is still much better than resigning yourself to doing all activities in a cumbersome and energy-draining whole-group format.

focus

SPLITTING OUT YOUR WORKSHOP

When planning in-person workshops, you're looking at durations from half a day up to two or three whole days for an offsite event. This just isn't practical online – the extra focus and concentration you need when working remotely makes it much more tiring.

We've found that the maximum amount of time a group can spend doing quality focused work is two hours at a stretch. This means you need to divide your workshops into smaller sections. Our rule of thumb is that every full-day workshop should be split into two or three blocks of up to two hours. There are huge benefits to working this way:

- you can set tasks to be completed in between the blocks
- you can engage teams in different time zones at different points in the process
- if your workshop is split over more than one day, you can take advantage of the fact that when people sleep their subconscious will get to work on the thoughts in their heads

One approach that works really well is to take the two-day offsite format and create a daily rhythm of workshops that runs over a week or two.

PLANNING FOR HYBRID WORKSHOPS

We're focusing mainly on workshops where all participants and facilitators join online. It's also possible to run workshops where some people are located together and others join individually from remote locations. Because these hybrid forms are neither one thing nor the other there's a risk they end up giving everyone a less than great experience. People who've travelled to offices may begrudge those who are working online, feeling they could have stayed at home. Remote participants could find their voices dominated by those in the physical room.

Just like remote workshops, the difference between a painful hybrid workshop and a productive and enjoyable one is careful planning and skilled facilitation. Follow these tips for a great participant experience and successful outcomes:

- Create an agenda with two tracks, one for online and one for in-person. Plan for moments where all participants are 'together' and for the rest of the time, create exercises and activities that run separately. As we'll show you over the next few pages, what works really well in person may be painful online and vice versa
- Put a facilitator with the participants in the physical room, dedicated to managing their conversation, exercises and timings
- Have a separate facilitator join remotely, dedicated to managing the online exercises, breakout rooms and timings
- Make sure there's a decent microphone in the workshop room so that the audio quality is clear for remote participants
- Where you have exercises that involve the whole group, get all participants to join from individual computers even if they're in the same space. It often works better for your participants to move to different spaces and use headphones even though this might feel odd
- Where you're voting to prioritise ideas or make decisions, ask all participants to do this on a polling tool on their phone or computer so you get a single tally
- For group activities, avoid mixing participants from the physical and online locations together in the same group

We've written this book as a guide to designing online workshops rather than a book of workshop exercises. There are already some great books out there on exercises – see the resources section and the Closer Apart website – and you'll find even more exercises available online from a quick internet search. The table below shows what type of exercises to search for to meet some common workshop objectives, and the names of just a few of our favourites.

WHEN YOU WANT TO...	SEARCH FOR...	OUR FAVOURITES...
Come up with new ideas	Ideation exercises	Crazy 8s 100 MPH thinking
Shift the energy of the group	Energisers	Treasure hunt Mindfulness
Get a team working well together	Team building exercises	Timeline Strengths and preferences
Solve problems	Problem-solving exercises	Problem tree 5 Whys
Create new vision	Visioning exercises	1-2-4-All Future Headline
Make decisions	Decision-making exercises	Impact-effort matrix SWOT analysis
Make plans	Planning exercises	SWOT analysis

ADAPTING YOUR
EXERCISES TO WORK ONLINE

A COMMON pitfall when planning remote workshops is to take formats that were designed to be run in person and simply shift them onto video calls. The main reasons this doesn't usually work are that the tech isn't appropriate and the energy can't be sustained for as long. We've seen half-day or even whole-day team-building workshops that almost destroyed the teams when moved online, because of the sheer amount of time participants were asked to spend looking at the screen.

Here are a few tips on timing and energy to help you as you take your workshop online:

- In any two-hour remote session you can complete a maximum of two detailed exercises. We suggest you run these in segments lasting no longer than 45 minutes each.

- Alternate longer and shorter exercises to keep participants engaged and energised

- Schedule a break roughly midway, ideally before a complex exercise so that people begin refreshed

When it comes to the actual exercises you use, most will work well online without many alterations but again, you need to give thought to timings and energy. You really can think big when designing or adapting exercises for remote workshops: take any exercise you like to use in a physical setting and reproduce it online. You can transfer text-based exercises onto shared documents, and where you would use sticky notes or paper canvases, transfer to a visual collaboration tool like Mural or Miro.

We designed and facilitated in-person workshops for 800 people working at a large manufacturing organisation, to help them co-create values. We had to split the workshop into 16 sessions for 50 people each, use a very large room, many rolls of whiteboard and thousands of sticky notes. When we took these workshops online, we had groups of 200 on Zoom so we only needed to run 4 sessions. To encourage everyone to engage with at least one other person and switch their camera on, we started with an exercise where we put

125

people into pairs in 100 breakout rooms before moving to co-creation in 40 rooms of 5 people. We included a guided meditation exercise to help participants focus and a treasure hunt to inject a real sense of energy and fun before the end. This shows just how much you can do when you think big – and how workshops online really can be even better than in person.

GIVING INSTRUCTIONS

One major difference when planning remote workshops is the level of detail you need when it comes to instructions. Your participants need to know exactly what to do each time they have to use technology during the workshop. You can't just gesture to your co-facilitator to go and help someone as you would when in a physical room together, so make sure everything is clearly spelled out. Create a clear script for introducing exercises and paste complex instructions into chat.

FACILITATOR TIP:

- ▇ Have a plan B for your most important exercises
- ▇ If co-facilitating, make sure that both facilitators can run any exercise in case one drops out
- ▇ If you've set pre-work, make a plan for what you'll do if people haven't completed it

CREATING YOUR AGENDA

Now that you've completed your planning canvas, what next? You might be tempted to jump straight into the workshop design but there's one more step – you need to create a detailed agenda. Doing this in a spreadsheet is a simple way to organise the timing information. There's a free Google and Excel spreadsheet on the Closer Apart website for you to copy or use for inspiration.

Your agenda should include:

- minute-by-minute timings
- roles and responsibilities – who's leading the exercise, who's responsible for the technology, who's taking notes etc
- instructions for the exercises, including timings
- scripts for introductions and explanations
- text for you to copy and paste into chat
- breakout-room participants
- links to collaborative documents or sites

Keep your agenda close to hand during the session, ideally in a separate window near the location of the webcam on your computer – this gives your participants the sense they have your full attention.

Create a summary agenda to give to your participants. This doesn't need to have all the fine detail above, only the exercise titles.

SPREADSHEET:
Download free Google
and Excel spreadsheets.

127

PLANNING is absolutely fundamental to a successful workshop. If you understand these key points about planning, and you follow the sequence laid out on the Planning Canvas, you're on a sure path to a fantastic workshop.

FACILITATOR TIP:

Present your agenda in a visual form. One example is the pie-chart style below. It's a great way to help people quickly understand what they'll work on.

EXAMPLE VISUAL AGENDA

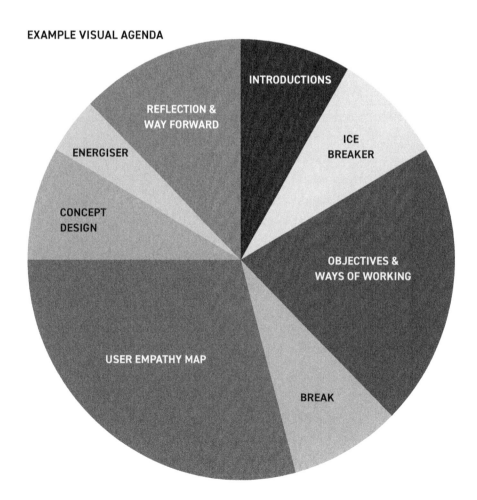

EXERCISE 7 – CONSIDER YOUR PARTICIPANTS

Ask yourself these questions about the workshop you're planning:

■ How do I want my participants to FEEL?

■ What do I want them to THINK?

■ What do I want them to DO?

THE WORKSHOP JOURNEY

THE WORKSHOP JOURNEY

BY now you're probably eager to get going and learn how to design and facilitate your own online workshop.

The workshop journey starts from the first conversation you have about the workshop and finishes when the final email is sent. Having the whole workshop journey in your mind helps you to see the full picture and identify missing components or elements you need to finesse. Often it's the little details that happen around a workshop that can make it brilliant instead of good.

The next five sections of the book break down the essential stages of the workshop journey:

- Before the workshop
- Beginnings
- Middles
- Endings
- After the workshop

Each stage of your workshop will have a specific purpose that requires an

appropriate energy level. We'll suggest ideas for different exercises, tools and managing energy at each stage and our expert guest facilitators will inspire you with ideas of their own. Remember that every exercise you plan will take the same form, with a beginning, a middle and an end.

There are thousands of tools available online, so we're not going to list each one here. You can find a treasure trove of inspiration and exercises on our list of our favourite resources at the end of the book and on the Closer Apart website.

Before we move on to the next section, this is a great moment for you to think about a workshop you're going to facilitate, or perhaps one you've run in the past that you'd love to improve for next time. Take a pen or pencil and fill in a blank copy of the Remote Workshop Planning Canvas as we go. You can look back at the instructions on page 114 if you need a reminder, or watch the video of the Planning Canvas being completed on the Closer Apart website.

BEFORE THE WORKSHOP

135

Your workshop doesn't start at 9am on the first morning. The activities you do in the weeks, days and hours before your participants arrive are crucial.

In this chapter, we'll give you a rundown of the main things to consider. If you already have your own 'must do' preparations, feel free to add them to your workshop checklist.

LOGISTICS

WHO'S going to do what on your facilitation
team? Do you have a co-facilitator? Do you
have tech support? Do you need somebody
to carry out administrative tasks like send
emails or organise calendars?

If you're facilitating for a client
organisation, try to establish a single
internal point of contact who can access
participants' calendars, coordinate, send
meeting invitations and answer queries.

CONNECT WITH YOUR PARTICIPANTS

THE more you know about your participants the better, and not just those you suspect might be challenging! If you understand how everyone's thinking and feeling, what needs they might have and what their hopes are for the workshop, you'll be able to guide your time together more successfully.

We suggest that before every workshop, you engage with everyone. If you're short on time or you have lots of participants, send out a quick survey (you'll need to build in time to review the results). If you have more time, one-to-one conversations are great for building trust and empathy. This is especially useful for high-stakes workshops where particular participants can have a significant impact on the outcome of the workshop; budget-holders, or very senior decision-makers, for example.

The following questions will prompt useful information, whether you ask them in a conversation or in a survey:

- What will make this workshop a success for you?
- Do you have any accessibility or dietary requirements (if you're sending food)?
- Is there anything else you'd like the facilitators to know?

SEND PRE-COMMUNICATIONS

CONTACT your participants again, listing everything they need to prepare beforehand or have with them on the day. We suggest you do this no earlier than one week before the workshop but leaving two or three days for people to prepare themselves and complete any tasks you give them.

If the workshop takes place over lunchtime, ask them to have some food ready. Remind them they'll need their laptop charger plugged in, and a glass of water next to them. Your workshop will be fast-paced; you don't want to people step away from their screen unless it's part of an exercise, and you want it to be a comfortable experience for them with no interruptions.

Here are some tips on what to include in your pre-workshop email:

- joining instructions: time, date, link to the meeting and any collaboration tools you'll be using
- links to video instructions for the technology you'll be using – all good tools have how-to videos, so save time

prepar

in the workshop by asking people to watch these in advance

■ a questionnaire inviting input to objectives and any other information you need

■ reminders of what to have to hand: water, snacks, pen and paper etc

■ instructions for any tasks to be completed before the workshop, such as pre-reading, watching videos, completing questionnaires etc

If you have the time and money, you could send out workshop kits in the post. When your participants receive the same sticky notes and pens, snacks to eat and drinks to make together, it can turn your workshop into a special event.

It's worth re-sending the key instructions the day before the event – never assume people will have read your first email!

WHEN TO CANCEL

IF key people have to pull out of the
workshop, in particular a critical decision-
maker, can you reshape it to achieve part of
the objective or something else of value?

If not, you might have no option but to
cancel or reschedule your workshop.
There's no latest point to cancel; going
ahead without the ingredients for success
risks wasting everyone's time.

THE DAY BEFORE

WITH just 24 hours to go you should have everything under control. This is the time to have a final run-through with your co-facilitator and any other team members.

Choose the outfit you're going to wear – even though many of us have let our work wardrobes shrink to loungewear or even pyjamas, your participants will appreciate it if you make an effort and show up well-dressed... even if only from the waist up! Pick clothes that look great on camera and make you feel comfortable in your own space; bright colours and simple patterns are very effective.

Similarly, check your backdrop on screen. Remove clutter, include some visual stimuli and ideally some plants. We're not big fans of virtual backgrounds as they can interfere with showing objects or drawings on paper, but they're good if you're in a space you'd rather people can't see.

To run a great workshop you need to have energy, and an online workshop demands more of you than a physical one – you don't have the energy of participants in the room to bounce off. Get a good night's sleep the night before if you can. It's a great idea to read through your agenda and any script notes just before bedtime so that your subconscious can run through it while you sleep. The power of the subconscious is often underestimated – harnessing it will put you in a good position the next morning.

ON THE DAY

THINK of your workshop as a performance: you need to put on a great show for your participants! Get some exercise if you can and eat a healthy breakfast or lunch before you start. If you're running energiser exercises, wear something practical.

Prepare your physical space: make sure your desk is tidy and you have everything you need to hand: a printed agenda (if you like to have a paper copy), pen and paper, water, coffee or tea and an emergency snack in case your energy starts to dip.

Check that all your software is updated and anything battery-operated is plugged in and fully charged – the last thing you need is for your laptop to start an unexpected upgrade or your phone to run out of charge at a critical moment. About 30 minutes before the workshop, start your video link.

If you're co-facilitating, arrange to meet your co-facilitator on the video link. Check each other's visibility, microphone and the quality of the connection. Walk through the agenda, making sure you're clear on who's doing what when, and particular risks you should watch out for. Doing this will establish the flow of the workshop clearly in your mind and help the session run smoothly.

After the run-through, turn off your camera, share your screen showing the welcome image if you're using one and play some music. Turn on 'Do Not Disturb' on your computer and turn your phone to silent mode.

Aim to finish the run-through 15 minutes before the scheduled start-time and take ten minutes to get physically and mentally 'in the zone'. Here are a few ideas for exercises you could build into your pre-workshop routine. Make it your own, and use it every time.

- go for a walk outside – fresh air and daylight have an instant effect on energy and mood
- stretch – especially your neck and shoulders, which can get very tense
- take a moment to close your eyes and take three deep breaths
- meditate for a few minutes with an app like Headspace
- perform some voice exercises to get your vocal cords warmed up
- adopt a pose that makes you feel confident – shoulders back!
- do 30 seconds of vigorous exercise like star jumps

Five minutes before the workshop starts, take a big stretch, roll your shoulders out a few times, sit down in front of your computer with an upright and confident posture, and smile. Turn on the camera – your curtain has lifted and the workshop has begun!

FACILITATOR TIP:
Here are a few tips to look after yourself. You can't help other people if you're struggling, so look after your own energy first!
- **set up your station with water and energy-giving snacks**
- **take a walk, move around or stretch**
- **take regular breaks, especially in longer workshops**
- **accept that something will probably go wrong, and if it does you have everything you need to adapt and carry on**

BEGINNINGS

The beginning of the workshop is when you establish your credibility, set the tone and create energy. Get it right and you'll lay the foundations for a brilliant workshop.

If people have problems logging in or getting audio and video set up, smile, breathe and stay calm – whatever happens, you're ready for it.

WELCOME!

THERE are many ways to welcome people into an online workshop. At Curve we like to balance professionalism and polish with a personal and welcoming atmosphere.

A few minutes before the workshop is scheduled to start, switch on your camera so you can welcome people by name and start to get a little bit of interaction going between your participants. You might want to set up a waiting room on your video platform so that participants gather individually in a neutral or branded space and you can admit them all together when you're ready.

Once everyone has entered the virtual room it's time to start building trust, both between facilitators and participants and between participants. Building trust is the foundation of psychological safety, and means people can take part without fear of negative consequences.

In psychologically safe workshops, participants feel accepted and respected. To enable this, it's important to show yourself as being human, for example by sharing some personal information (humorous stories are a bonus), smiling and using hand gestures. You can build on a simple first action like this by explaining how you'll keep the workshop safe and by demonstrating kindness and care for your participants.

Introduce the technology you'll be using as soon as you can. Encourage participants to use the chat function to ask for help so that a co-facilitator or tech support person can deal with these requests without taking your attention away from the whole group.

GIVING INSTRUCTIONS

CREATE a script for introductions to exercises, especially those with multiple steps. Make sure your instructions are clear, speak them slowly and, where possible, give them twice. At the end of the second explanation, ask the group if they've understood and to raise their thumbs if they have or wave if they haven't. If you get many waves, explain again. If it's just one or two people, then your co-facilitator can help them separately or you can join their group to clarify. It's best not to disrupt the whole group with an explanation most people already understand just to meet the needs of one or two people.

You can also type the instructions into the chat so that people can read them in their own time – write them into your agenda in advance, or into a separate document so you can copy and paste them quickly. If you're using a collaboration tool such as Google Docs or Mural, write the instructions here as well. This is especially helpful if anyone has English as their second language.

FACILITATOR TIP:

Here's an example of instruction text you could place in the shared document or chat and a script for how you could introduce it:

Task: Come up with a name and mission statement for your team

Timing: 5 minutes

*Team Name: _Insert your team name here_*

*Mission Statement: _Insert your mission statement here_*

Script: "For this exercise I'm going to split you into four teams: (name the people in the teams). You're going to have five minutes to come up with a name and mission statement for your team. When you return to the main room, I'm going to ask one person at random from each team to present their name and why they chose it."

WE'VE noticed that people are less inclined to ask for help in a remote setting, so giving good instructions is critical to your success, especially when your group is split into teams working without a facilitator. Make sure people know how to ask for help from a breakout room. Most platforms have functions to call for help or send messages and even if yours doesn't, you can suggest participants use email or an instant messaging tool. Once your instructions are clear and the teams are happy, set them onto their tasks with enthusiasm and a big smile!

WAYS OF WORKING

A GREAT way to establish trust is to run an exercise to identify the ways of working for the session. You'll note that we don't use the term 'rules' because, in our experience, the more you give people rules to abide by, the more they'll try to get around them! In a Ways of Working exercise you can open up a conversation about how the group would like to work together. We suggest allowing the group to create and document its own ways of working. You can suggest topics to include such as:

- confidentiality
- avoiding distractions
- any planned interruptions like scheduled calls
- having fun
- accepting and building on each other's ideas
- criticising concepts and not people

FACILITATOR TIP:
If you have specific concerns you'd like the group to address in the Ways of Working, ask one of the participants you get along well with to bring them up. For example, if you know people are easily distracted, ask them to suggest everyone agrees to close email and turn off notifications.

Ways of Working has the effect of transferring authority and power from the facilitator to the participant. They're not *your rules*, they're *our ways of working*.

If during the workshop you find that behaviour is deviating from the agreed ways of working, you can gently refer people back to them and ask if they need to be changed. This often has the immediate effect of putting a stop to challenging behaviour!

ICEBREAKERS AND WARMUPS

ICEBREAKERS and warmups are critical to the start of any great workshop. They're often overlooked in online workshops, which is especially problematic as you need them even more where you lose the spontaneous encounters that usually help people get to know each other. In many ways icebreakers and warmups are similar: they help the group to build a level of trust, empathy and energy to embark on the work that needs to be done. Their differences lie in their references to different temperatures!

Icebreakers are typically used where the group hasn't met one another or where there is tension. The ice needs to be broken so that ideas can begin to move.

In groups who are used to working together or where a level of trust has already been established, there's no ice to be broken. You'll just need to warm up to get the juices flowing again.

A well-designed and well-chosen opening activity creates a level of energy, injects a sense of fun and introduces participants to one another. In his book, *Social Physics*, *Alex Pentland* describes the concept of conversational turn-taking. He found that the more equal the share of voice in any group, the more collective intelligence the group will have, so the better the ideas they'll generate.

Also, it's been proven that the earlier people speak in a meeting or workshop, the more likely they are to contribute later on. This effect is even more pronounced for minority groups and for women, so it's really important you make sure everyone has the opportunity to speak as early as possible.

trust

INTRODUCTIONS

YOUR participants need to know who's attending the workshop with them, especially if they're not a pre-existing team. If you're an external facilitator working in a client organisation, don't assume all participants will know each other; there are always new joiners and in large organisations it would be impossible to know everyone. Good introductions will make sure everybody's voice is heard, allow every participant to share a small personal story and create the sense of a team coming together. This ensures your workshop has a positive start.

Try to avoid introduction exercises that encourage people to share job titles or career history. As soon as job titles enter the room, you inject hierarchy, which can really get in the way of collaboration in workshops. And job titles aren't that interesting; anybody who wants to know this information can easily go to LinkedIn or the company directory. Here are some ideas for introduction prompts you can use:

- what's one moment of joy you've had in the past month?
- what's your favourite place to visit and why?

- what mistake have you made that you've learned most from?
- what's the best piece of advice you've ever been given?
- share something surprising or interesting about yourself

We love to create introduction exercises where people speak to one another in pairs and then present back the information they've learned about their partner. Firstly, it means everyone will have had at least one meaningful conversation with another participant early on in your workshop – everyone in the room now has at least one friend. Secondly, it removes any anxiety people have around speaking about themselves and allows them to pay attention to the other people being introduced instead. There's no need for anyone to 'rehearse' their lines in advance.

If you have a very large group and want to encourage a sense of connection between the participants, ask simple questions and get participants to respond in the chat function. It's energising to see the responses as they flood in. You can also use tools like Slido or Mentimeter to turn responses into engaging live word clouds.

REVIEW AND SET OBJECTIVES

EVEN though you covered the objectives when you took the workshop brief and filled in the planning canvas, it's still important to spend time discussing the objectives at the start. You'll make sure everyone has the opportunity to contribute, gain buy-in from your participants and validate your workshop plan.

People often ask us, "But what if somebody brings an objective I haven't planned for?" That's a valid question but, in our experience, it's important you understand what everybody wants out of the workshop. You can either adjust your plans or suggest that the objective is dealt with in some other way. Otherwise, the unspoken objective might be declared in the final minutes when you have no ability to deal with it. This risks bringing your well-planned workshop to an unsatisfactory close.

If someone raises an objective you aren't expecting, you have a few options. If it's possible to meet the objective with only minor changes, you can think on your feet and incorporate it into the design of the workshop. If it needs significant changes to be made, ask the whole group whether they feel it's important and if it is, call a short break or send participants to breakout rooms while you make a new plan with your co-facilitator and sponsor. If it's clear this new objective can't be met, thank the person who suggested it and propose that you meet after the session to work out how to meet it – perhaps this could be the beginning of a brief for a whole new workshop!

DESCRIBE THE WORKSHOP JOURNEY AND AGENDA

NOW you're ready to get the group thinking about the work to be done. Your participants will be eager to find out what's in store for them and you need to start moving through what's always a very packed agenda.

Always start by talking your group through the different activities you've planned and how these will help the group meet its stated objectives. Use visuals to support your verbal run-through so that participants absorb and understand the information. These visuals could be:

■ A simple bullet list or table
■ A visual agenda – look back at the pie chart example in the planning section

■ A sketch of the journey like the one opposite
■ If you're working on a shared whiteboard with spaces for each of your exercises you can share this on your screen as you talk through the agenda

However you present what's to come, this is your opportunity to enthuse and inspire your participants!

We advise that you keep the timings of individual exercises to yourself so that you can flex them if you need to. Do tell the group when you plan to have breaks though, so they can relax if they have urgent emails or phone calls to fit in.

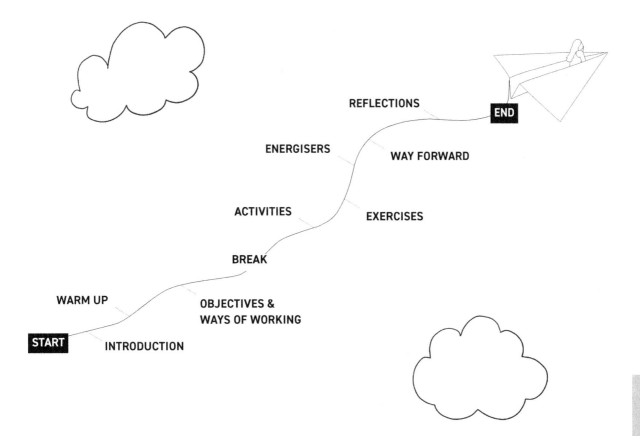

START
INTRODUCTION
WARM UP
OBJECTIVES &
WAYS OF WORKING
BREAK
ACTIVITIES
EXERCISES
ENERGISERS
WAY FORWARD
REFLECTIONS
END

ROLL UP YOUR SLEEVES

THE ground for your workshop is now well
prepared. Your objectives and ways of
working have been agreed, your participants
know and trust one another, they have faith
in your ability as a facilitator and they love
the look of their workshop journey. It's time
to invite them to start the first exercise.

MANY BEGINNINGS

YOU'LL usually need to split online
workshops into multiple parts so that
you can manage screen fatigue and maintain
focus. This means you'll have a beginning
at the start of every session. Treat the start
of every exercise as a mini-beginning,
remembering that how you speak and
move will set the energy and tone for
what's to follow.

focus

165

MIDDLES

The middle of the workshop is its heart. It's the place where the work gets done, where the group creates new ideas and builds momentum for change.

The shape and size of the middle varies immensely from workshop to workshop depending on what you want to achieve.

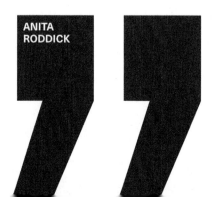

"What I have learned is that people become motivated when you guide them to the source of their own power.

ANITA RODDICK

170

BUILDING THE MIDDLE

FOR some workshops, the middle could be half an hour of ideation to come up with a new concept. In other workshops you could be working over many days to absorb information and inspiration, understand audience behaviour, develop manifestos and visions and build team behaviours.

Your job as facilitator is to think carefully about the outputs and outcomes for the overall workshop and build a middle section that will deliver them. In the middle part of any workshop, the burden of work should sit mainly with participants.

Don't get drawn into doing the work for them! Instead, use your energy to explain the processes, guide them to their own solutions and encourage them to take their ideas further.

GROUP WORK AND CHECKING IN

IN the middle of your workshop, you'll often send your participants into smaller groups to complete exercises over fairly long stretches of time. Your clear instructions at the beginning will set them off on the right course – now you have to make sure they stay on track and keep moving forward.

When you're using breakout rooms or separate parallel virtual meetings for small group work, it's harder to see how the group's progressing. In a physical meeting room you'd be able to look across and spot the group that's arguing about the task or joking around instead of getting on with the exercise. Online you're blind to these dynamics unless you're constantly popping into each breakout room, which can be disruptive for the teams.

You have other options; if you're using a shared document or space for collaboration, you'll be able to see changes in real time as the teams get work done. It usually takes a while for a group to get going but if one group lags behind others then you can drop in once to their breakout room to see if they need help.

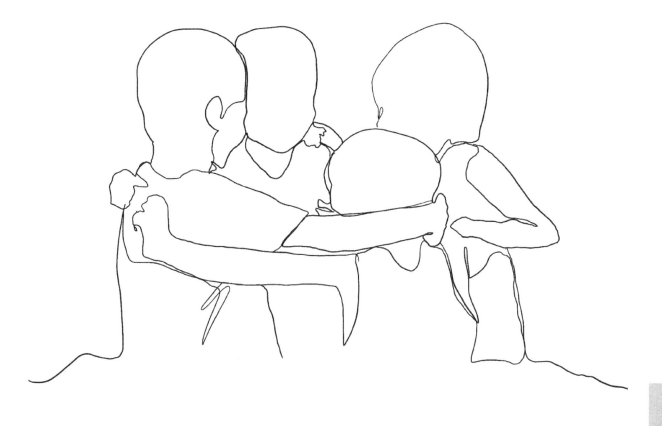

QUIET TIME AND TIMINGS

IF you're using breakout rooms, the point when your teams start working in their groups will be the first moment you have to yourself. In our experience, the additional stress of dealing with technology in online workshops means you might arrive at this point feeling slightly flustered.

If you're working with a co-facilitator, check in on each other to see how it's going, and give a boost of support or energy if needed. Check the agenda to see how you're progressing against your timings.

Think of timings in a workshop as elastic rather than rigid. Flex them to allow more time on exercises that are proving really valuable and save time by shortening activities where the group is making rapid progress. Keep the overall agenda in mind to make sure you're going to hit your objective in the time you have, but it's fine to add or subtract a few minutes as you work through the exercises. Activities often take longer than planned, especially if you have a talkative group. There are three actions you can take if you're over-running:

- shorten individual exercises – you can make this invisible to your participants
- limit the number of people who report back on an exercise
- have a single exercise that you can cut entirely if you need to bring yourself back on track

A workshop that ends halfway through an exercise or feels rushed at the end doesn't make for a great experience for you or your participants.

elastic

FACILITATOR TIP:

Don't worry if your workshop is running slightly ahead of time. End the workshop early and let your participants leave; they'll appreciate you giving them time at the end to get ready for their next call or energise themselves – it demonstrates empathy from you and helps people leave on a positive note.

ESCAPING THE ENERGY TROUGH

PAY special attention to energy levels in the middle of the workshop. You're asking your participants to do the hardest work here, to think deeply and interact with each other in ways that can uncover differences of opinion. You might encounter screen fatigue where your participants notice their eyes becoming sore or their shoulders and hips starting to ache. You're likely approaching the middle of the day where people's natural energy levels dip, or the post-lunch period when their energy is redirected to their stomachs.

To keep your workshop running smoothly, introduce energisers at this point. Remember what you've learned about energy: the human body and mind runs on it and your group will produce more and better work when their energy level is high.

The best way to raise energy is through physical movement. This can be vigorous star jumps or a gentle roll of the shoulders. You'll need to be firmly directive here! Everyone knows that moving physically is important when sitting at a desk all day, but when you encourage people to stand up and stretch, they'll often just nod and smile! Give them clear instructions and model the movement yourself.

When you want to create a calm energy or help participants connect to their emotions, introduce grounding energisers using slow movement. You can also lead guided breathing exercises – just three minutes of collective connection to the body and breath can completely shift the energy of the group (you could also show a mindfulness exercise from an app or YouTube).

> **FACILITATOR TIP:**
>
> Clients, especially those in senior roles, often say, "We don't have time for an energiser. We have so much work to get through, let's just press ahead". Explain to them that productivity is related to energy levels and point out that your exercise will only take a few minutes. At all costs, *keep the energisers*. They are the fuel your participants need to do their best work. When you've completed the energiser, ask the group to notice how their energy level has changed. The moment of reflection demonstrates how important it is to look after their own energy.

BRAIN WALKS

RUNNING an online workshop needn't mean sitting still in front of a screen all day – far from it! Experienced facilitators understand the benefits of getting their participants moving and out into the fresh air, and there's no reason you can't incorporate these exercises into an online workshop.

One of our favourite exercises combines movement and mindfulness through walking, inspired by the brilliant social enterprise, Street Wisdom. David Pearl founded this global social venture to bring what he calls 'the neuroscience of walking and creativity' together with beautifully simple questions in WalkShops.

Send participants to walk in their outdoor environment for 10-15 minutes with a specific challenge in mind. Tell them to ask themselves, "What do I hear? What do I see? What do I feel?" and to take inspiration from what they notice. You'd be surprised by the parallels the mind can draw from watching pigeons squabble over a piece of bread, or from the intricate veins in a leaf.

Help your participants avoid the temptation to skip the walk, switch off their camera and tackle a few emails by asking them to take a photo of something on the walk that's inspired them or that's related to the workshop topic.

SPOTLIGHT ON

Innovator in Business, the Arts and Social Change
DAVID PEARL

Talking about
WALKSHOPS

"Wayfinding requires that we become 'explorers of our world' seeking to discover and shine light upon that which is not seen.

DR CHELLIE SPILLER

CANVASES

PEOPLE think and work best when they're given structure. For this reason we love to create canvases – templates that guide the thinking process.

The phrase 'start with a blank page' is meant to sound encouraging but in our experience it can create a block. People don't know how and where to start when faced only with white space. The Curve Remote Workshop Planning Canvas we showed you earlier is one example of a canvas. Others we like to use include the Empathy Map Canvas that helps participants understand their users, and the Business Model Canvas to help participants map out the features of a new product or concept. You can find examples on the Closer Apart website or from a quick internet search. Remember, you can always create your own canvases by amending these or by starting from scratch.

As well as helping your participants to think during the workshop, a well-designed canvas will serve as a useful reference for work after the workshop. One of the huge benefits of remote workshops is that with a good canvas, almost all the typing up has been done for you by your participants!

SPOTLIGHT ON

Philosopher
KARIM BENAMAR

Talking about
REFRAMING

At the end of the workshop you want all the threads to come together to weave a beautiful tapestry with no loose ends. You want your participants to feel proud of the work they've done and a sense of ownership.

The momentum you've created together should carry the work forward and see that commitments made are honoured.

"

I've learned that people will forget what you said, people will forget what you did, but people will never forget how you made them feel.

MAYA ANGELOU

"

THE WORKSHOP *IS* THE WORK

THE energy at the end of the workshop should be at least as high as it was at the start. This is no mean feat! As a facilitator, you'll have been pouring your energy into the workshop since before it even started and by now, the chances are you'll be feeling pretty tired. But even if you're flagging, this is the moment for you to make the final push – the success of your workshop is disproportionately affected by what happens in the final few minutes. This chapter gives you a few simple tools to make sure your workshop finishes on a high.

THE WHOLE IS
MORE THAN
THE SUM OF
ITS PARTS

THERE'S an approach in psychology called
Gestalt. Beautifully explained in *The Fertile
Void:* Gestalt Coaching at Work by John
Leary-Joyce, it holds that human beings
are naturally drawn to see things balanced,
unified and coherent. People are drawn like
magnets to closure. The simplest example
of this is on the opposite page.
What do you see when you look at it?

whole

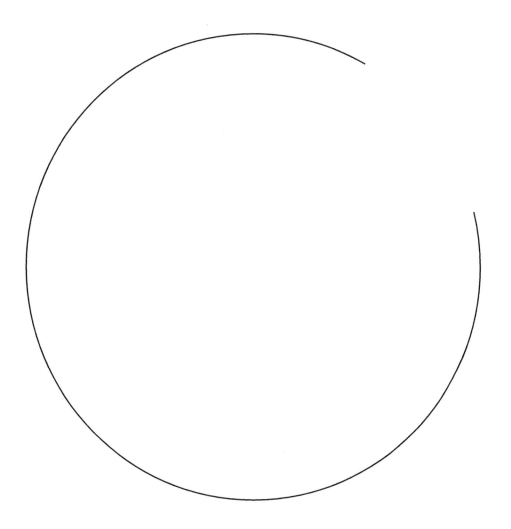

Most people say they see a circle, perhaps with a hole in it. In fact, it's just a line; it's the human mind that wants the ends to join to form a complete circle.

You can use this in your workshop. If you can draw the incomplete circle of the workshop journey in your participants' minds, they'll naturally want to close it and make it whole. When the whole becomes clear, your participants will leave the session with a sense of satisfaction and completion.

Start by returning to the objectives you set at the start of the workshop, share your screen and show the document or board where you recorded them. From there, summarise all the activities the group has completed during the workshop by looking back at your agenda and talking through what's been achieved. Even better, if you're using a visual collaboration tool, zoom out so that your group can see all the work they've done and how it fits together.

If the workshop has run over multiple sessions, make it clear which exercises happened in which sessions, on which days.

"
The way to achieve your own success is to be willing to help somebody else get it first.

IYANLA VANZANT

"

CONNECT THE WORKSHOP TO THE WORK THAT FOLLOWS

IT'S tempting to think of a workshop as
something separate from the work people
do day-to-day. But the best workshops are
both tightly integrated into business as
usual, and an opportunity to make step
changes and imagine radically different
futures. As you come to the close of your
workshop, explain how the work the group
has done will be carried forward. Tell them
what will happen next and when. Describe
any future sessions and how they'll be
involved in further phases of work.

REFLECT AND LEARN

AT the end of the workshop your goal is to have clear and comprehensive outputs that meet the objectives, and a group of people who feel energised about what they've done, excited about the future and committed to taking personal action to turn it all into success. A common pitfall that could well sabotage your goal is to close the workshop with a section called 'Actions and Next Steps'. You want your participants to finish by feeling motivated and energised rather than burdened with more work to do, especially as they'll likely return to full inboxes and long to-do lists. Plan your workshop to capture actions as you work through the exercises, designing a section of your collaborative documents or whiteboard to record them. Cover next steps in the summary of the workshop and agree how outputs will be carried forward.

After this is done, close the whole session in a positive and inspiring way by inviting your participants to reflect on the entire experience of the workshop. Encourage them to think more metaphorically and less in terms of practicalities. In most workshops, you spend the majority of the time working with words and language. Reflection using a visual stimulus is a great way to help your participants think differently and helps them to access their feelings about the workshop.

Try it yourself now. Look at the images printed on the opposite page. Which one represents how you feel about facilitating remote workshops having got this far in the book? Take a moment to write down your response to it.

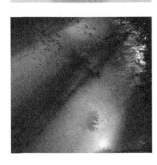

AFTER THE WORKSHOP

Facilitation is emotionally and energetically draining. By the end of your workshop you'll hopefully be on an adrenaline high with a huge sense of achievement.

You might also feel depleted after all the energy you put into building momentum, managing tensions and dealing with the potholes technology put in your way.

TIME TO RECHARGE

WHEN you're running online workshops there's no travel time to or from your virtual venue, and it's easy to end up with another meeting or perhaps even another workshop immediately afterwards. Make sure this doesn't happen – give yourself time to breathe and recharge.

Our advice is that if you're running more than one workshop session on any given day, it will take another day for you to be back on your best form, so try not to plan anything too demanding. If you can, delegate follow-up actions to other members of your team.

FEEDBACK

ALL great facilitators are constantly looking for ways to improve their workshops and their skills. The best way for you to do this is to get clear and candid feedback from participants, your workshop sponsor and your team. Ask them for feedback with this simple three-question format we like to use at Curve:

■ What did you like about the session?

■ What would you like more of?

■ What questions do you still have?

Send these to your participants as a feedback questionnaire. You can have this prepared in advance and ready to go out with your thank you email.

Spend five minutes at the end of your workshop checking in with your co-facilitators and other members of your team, asking them the same questions to get some instant feedback. Do this immediately after the workshop even though you might not feel like it. By the next day some of the really important insights may have been forgotten.

Schedule a time to reconvene with your co-facilitator and your client to run through the session and get feedback in more detail at a later point when you've recharged.

LET'S TRY THE FEEDBACK PROCESS RIGHT NOW.

Cast your mind back to a workshop that you've run or attended recently.

Answer the three feedback questions above.

"

If everything was perfect you would never learn and you would never grow.

BEYONCÉ
KNOWLES

"

FOLLOW-UP

YOUR final interaction with your workshop participants is likely to be a follow-up email. It's good to remind them of what they achieved and the momentum they built up, and to set out actions and next steps going forward. The following checklist has some suggestions for what to include:

- A copy of the digital outputs created on the day
- Screenshots of the group engaged in activities
- Recordings of presentations
- A list of actions and next steps
- A link to a feedback survey
- Your contact details for any questions or suggestions
- Tools, links or introductions you promised to send people during the session

If you're an external facilitator and the workshop went well (of course it did!), this is the best moment for you to plant the seeds for future work. Meet with your client, ask them what they liked about the workshop and how you might be able to help them further. If you get some great feedback, ask if you can use it as a client testimonial.

SPOTLIGHT ON

Co-founder and CEO of Amazing If
HELEN TUPPER

Talking about
FEEDBACK

PAUSE AND REFLECT

IN these five chapters we've spanned the whole arc of running a great workshop, from preparatory activities, sending pre-communications and getting yourself ready, to the moment you open your virtual room. We've looked at how you shape the beginning, middle and end of your workshop to balance the needs for inspiration, concentration and momentum, and what to do after the workshop.

Before we move on, it's time to facilitate yourself again and reflect on what you've learned. One of the most powerful yet simple questions to ask in a workshop is, "What is your aha from this exercise?" It helps participants to reflect and comment on what they've discovered and any surprises they've encountered, and whether the exercise was easy or hard. The responses can often take the workshop in unexpected and useful directions.

Let's try it now. Pause for a moment. Think back over the five chapters you've just read and reflect on the question opposite. Write down your answer – keep going if you have more than one. The more you reflect and write here, the more you'll remember and put into practice. Revisit the workshop plan you're working on and make any changes that could improve it.

Lovely! Thank you.

You are BRILLIANT! And now you have everything you need to design and run your own successful online workshops. The 'Good to Great' chapter at the end of the book gives you more tips to take your practice to the next level.

EXERCISE 8 – PRACTISE REFLECTION

What's your aha about how to run remote workshops?

"

Just try new things. Don't be afraid. Step out of your comfort zones and soar.

MICHELLE OBAMA

"

GOOD TO GREAT

WHAT you've learned so far will give you everything you need to plan and run a really good workshop. In this final chapter we're going to give you some tips to make your workshop not just really good, but great.

This is just the beginning though: there's always more to learn about design and facilitation. We're constantly improving our practice with inspiration from books, blogs and podcasts, and from watching and talking to other great facilitators. Visit the Closer Apart website and join our community – we'd love to see you there!

JOIN US:
Join our community
for more books, blogs
and podcasts.

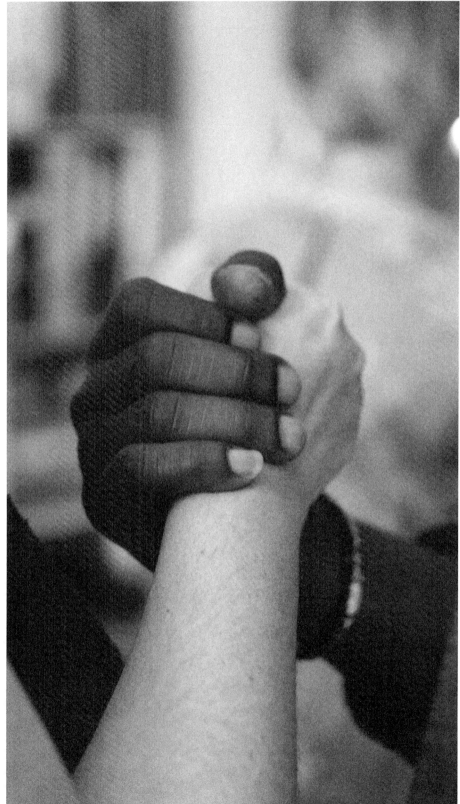

BUILDING YOUR OWN TOOLS

IN this book we've included spotlights from some of the world's best facilitators and coaches to give you ideas and inspiration for building your own exercises and we're always adding more to the website. Exercises work best when you know they've been tried and tested and tailored to the needs of your particular audience. Good is an exercise that meets their needs adequately. Great is one that fits them perfectly, adapted to make sure it meets their specific objectives. Here's a simple example to illustrate how you can adapt an exercise. One of our favourite exercises for coming up with lots of new ideas fast is called '100mph thinking'. You give participants a very short amount of time to come up with as many ideas as they can. It was introduced to us by Mark Prince who wrote our foreword. If Mark were running a workshop for Formula One, for example, he might adapt it by changing the title to '400mph thinking'. Just this tiny adjustment would make it clear to his client that Mark was alert to their specific context and needs.

COACHING

COACHING is a practice that's widely used in the world of business and in many other areas of life. At the heart of the coaching approach is the idea that every individual has what they need within themselves to be successful. The coach uses tools and approaches to unlock that potential. The approach is even more powerful when you apply it to groups, with the potential multiplied by the number of participants.

You can introduce coaching techniques into your workshop to great effect. Here are a few of the simplest and most powerful:

Active Listening

This is the process of listening attentively while someone else speaks. Nod and smile to show that you're following. Mirror body language, paraphrase and reflect back what you've heard, withholding judgment and advice.

Silence

Sometimes when you ask a question of your group, you're met with silence. This could be because your participants haven't understood your question, but it might be that they're thinking through the answer. Avoid the temptation to dive in straight away with more questions. You might have asked a really powerful and provocative question. Leaving silence allows space for your participants to process their thoughts and reach their breakthrough.

Tell me more...

This is possibly the most powerful phrase in the facilitator's lexicon. When you encounter something in the workshop that sparks curiosity or is potentially threatening or challenging, the open question, "tell me more", invites your participant to open up and respond in a constructive way.

SPOTLIGHT ON

Author of the bestseller *The Coaching Habit*
MICHAEL BUNGAY STANIER

Talking about
THE AWE QUESTION

more

IMPROVISATION

THE best facilitators are great improvisers. The art of improvising is taking something that already exists and 'riffing' on it, like a jazz musician who collaborates and builds on the ideas of the other players to create wonderful, unique melodies.

One approach that's often used in improv theatre is the phrase, 'Yes, and...' By starting with this phrase every time, the performers add energy and build on each other's ideas. The same follows for suggestions made in a workshop. If, on the other hand, the response to ideas is 'Yes, but...', you block new thinking, provoke challenge and remove energy.

An improvisational mindset is really important in workshops. If you're able to adapt or improvise when something unexpected happens, you can quickly pivot and take advantage of suggestions from participants on how to improve the session. When something goes wrong, you'll feel empowered to make changes instead of worrying about losing control. If you adopt an improvisational mindset, your participants will too. The more they embody the spirit and practice of 'Yes, and...', the sooner the ideas will start flowing.

VISUALISE YOUR WORKSHOP

MANY sportspeople use visualisation techniques to prepare for competitions. The superstar Brazilian footballer, Pelé, famously took an hour before every game to find a quiet place in the locker room and lie down to visualise success. In this routine he would play a 'movie' of his entire football career in his head. The movie began with Pelé playing football as a child and ended with a montage of the best moments of his career in multiple World Cup finals. He brought to mind strong emotions of joy and fun from the past to set the emotional tone for the upcoming game.

EXERCISE 9 – VISUALISE IT

Close your eyes and try to visualise your workshop, moment by moment. Step through the agenda in your mind as it's going to happen. What will you say? How will your participants react? What will the outputs be? How will the energy feel?

Try and be as detailed as you can when imagining the workshop, bringing to mind the feelings you'll experience.

HOW FAR COULD YOU TAKE IT?

ANOTHER brilliant technique from the world of coaching is called the 'magic wand question' where you ask yourself, "If you had a magic wand, if there were no barriers, what would you do?"

Let's apply that question to your workshop. Imagine if there were no constraints; if you could do anything, what would you do? Who would be there? Would you have graphic artists making live illustrations of the discussions as they happen? Dancers and musicians? Would you try to stage a TV-style talent show?

Who would your keynote speakers be? What technology would you use? What technology would you create that doesn't even exist yet?

The further you take this magic wand idea the more likely you are to come up with exciting ideas. And once you've got exciting ideas you can think about how to hack some version of them together. The human mind is incredibly powerful at coming up with innovative solutions – and of course you could run a mini-workshop to work out how to do it!

HOW BIG CAN YOU GO?

WHEN facilitating online there's almost
no theoretical limit to the size of your
workshop. In principle you could welcome
every single internet-connected human
on the planet. Why you would want to is
another matter, but even the idea shows
the exciting potential of online facilitation.
Just remember, the more participants
you have, the bigger your facilitation team
needs to be.

YES, YOU CAN!

WE hope you've learned a lot from reading this book, from exploring the content and spotlights on the website and from working your way through the exercises. Hopefully you discovered not just practical tips but some new knowledge about yourself and what kind of facilitator you might be. Remember that the sooner you put your new knowledge into action the more effective it will be. Look for an opportunity to design and run a workshop as soon as you can. Good luck and have fun!

EXERCISE 10 – TOMORROW I WILL...

The sooner you put new skills and knowledge into practice, the more likely you are to remember them and use them over time. You'll also build your confidence if you start now. Not starting is the single biggest way to prevent the change you want to make in your life. We love to finish workshops by doing this very simple exercise:

What one small action are you going to take to put what you've learned today into practice tomorrow?

Answer it now...

Tomorrow I will...

WHAT NEXT?

THERE are lots of ways to learn facilitation skills with Curve, from self-paced online courses to facilitator-led training in a live workshop setting. Use this QR code to find full details of all our learning resources and special discounts for readers of Closer Apart.

   Our mantra at Curve is, "We like people, we love to talk, we want to help". We'd love to hear from you.

John & Lizzie

 CLOSER APART:
Find full details of all our learning resources and special discounts.

HOW CURVE
CAN HELP YOU

CURVE is a creative leadership company. Through facilitation, coaching and leadership development, we help individuals, teams and organisations to create their own change.

To find out more or book us to speak at your event, visit our website, www.curve.cc

If you'd like to order this book in bulk, or if you'd like us to customise or co-brand it for your organisation, talk to us at hello@curve.cc.

OTHER BOOKS TO HELP YOU

Pamela Hamilton, *The Workshop Book*

Lisette Sutherland, *Work Together Anywhere*

Dave Gray, *Gamestorming*

Brene Brown, *Dare to Lead*

Michael Bungay Stanier, *The Coaching Habit*

Kim Scott, *Radical Candor*

Kim Scott, *Just Work*

Daniel Kahneman, *Thinking Fast and Slow*

Christina Wodtke, *Radical Focus*

Daniel Stillman, *The 30 Second Elephant and the Paper Airplane Experiment: Origami for Design Thinking*

Michelle Howard, *Lessons from the Trough*

Karin M. Reed and Joseph A. Allen, *Suddenly Virtual*

Pilar Orti, *Thinking Remote*

Priya Parker, *The Art of Gathering*

Karim Benamar, *Reframing – The Art of Thinking Differently*

Adam Grant, *Think Again*

The Power of Facilitation, *Kimberly Bain*

GRATITUDE

WE'D like to close this final page with some thanks and appreciation, and give one last thing to you in doing so.

Research shows that if you practise gratitude, you're much more likely to have a greater sense of happiness and wellbeing. Taking regular moments to be thankful will also make you healthier by boosting your immune system. With so many people we'd like to thank for helping to get this book out into the world, we're all but guaranteed to be happy and healthy for a long time to come!

Thanks to Bruce Daisley for inspiring us at his own book launch – this journey began the very next day. To Cate Caruth for helping to plan out the book and keep it on track over many months. To Anthea Morrison for wresting the language from beast into beauty. To Fern Miller for the inspired book title. To George Walkley for publishing guidance. To Nic Howell and Johnnie Moore for the original inspiration. To Hazel and Dave Graham for the book and website design. To Alison Booth for endlessly can-do support.

Huge gratitude also to Bonnie, Rachel, Inga, Lawrence and Lisa from the Curve team for their ideas, support and problem-solving. Finally, thank you Michael Bungay Stanier for this great idea to reframe acknowledgements into these much more friendly 'gratitudes'.

You're all brilliant!

CLOSING EXERCISE

Take a moment now and write down three things you're grateful for.

1

2

3

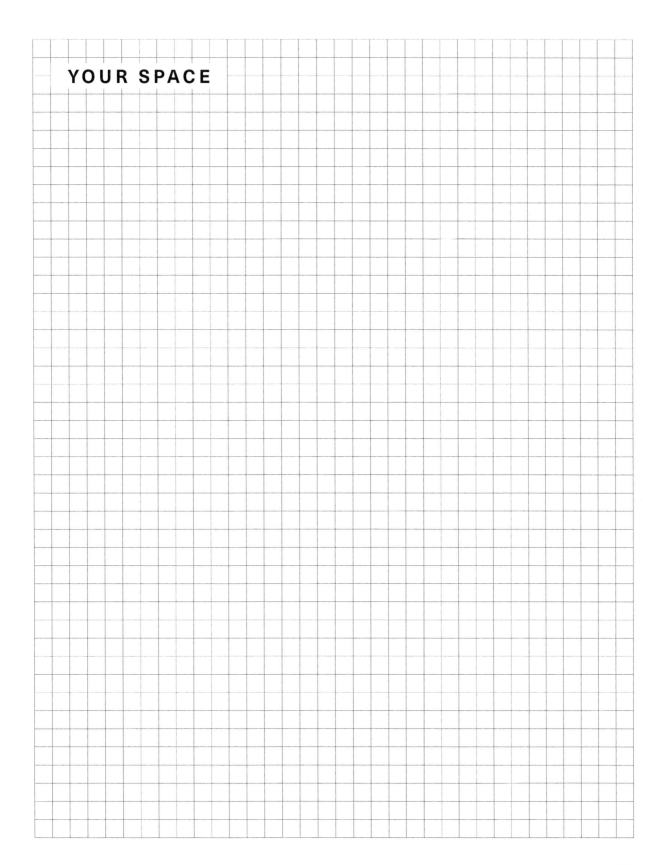

YOUR SPACE

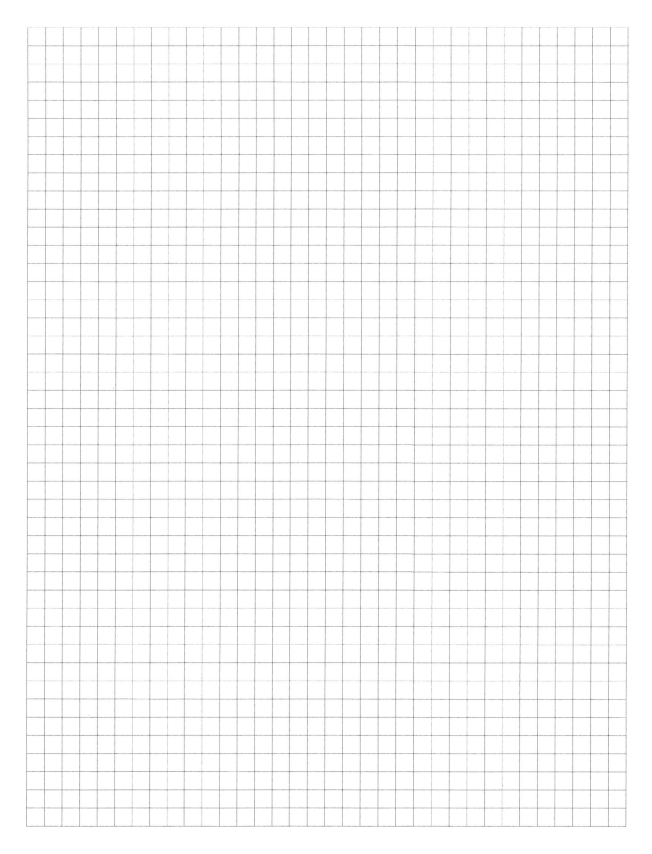

Printed in Great Britain
by Amazon